The
Bride
of
Christ

The Bridegroom and His Bride

Christopher W. Hussey

ISBN 978-1-63575-845-0 (Paperback)
ISBN 978-1-63575-846-7 (Digital)

Christian Faith Publishing, Inc.
296 Chestnut Street
Meadville, PA 16335
www.christianfaithpublishing.com

Printed in the United States of America

CONTENTS

DEDICATION

To my wife Jamie of twenty-nine years. Your loyalty and love is no doubt a reflection of your pursuit of God.

To my children, Anna and her husband Ryan, Josh, Kate, and Nate, you are all such a blessing in my life.

To Skylar my granddaughter, you are such a precious gift from God. I trust there will be many more that follow.

ACKNOWLEDGEMENTS

I want to thank my spiritual sister Barbara Colacchia for putting my words onto paper. Your love and friendship has been an incredible joy in my life.

I also want to thank Pastor Nataly Galichansky, Pastor Troy Bramblet, the elders and the congregation of Abundant Life Community Church, for your love and all the words of encouragement. They have been a source of life to me!

INTRODUCTION

The Bride of Christ is one of the seven figures of the church that describes the way the church responds and reacts to the Lord Jesus Christ. The way that the bride of Christ is to respond to Christ is in a deep, affectionate, love, and intimate relationship with Him. It is not about religion; it is about an intimate walk. It is about a relationship of love. It's about companionship and fellowship. Let me assure you that as deep as this love is between Christ and His bride, it is not a sexual love. Jesus is the lover of our souls. The love of God goes so far deeper than any human love possibly can.

In Ephesians 3, Paul prays that the believers would know and understand the length, breath, depth, and the height of God's love, which surpasses knowledge, that they may be filled up with all the fullness of God. The word "know" in this passage is not a head knowledge, it is an experiential knowledge. Paul is praying that the people of God would experience the fullness of God's love in a tangible, manifested way that absolutely transforms their lives.

When you are touched by God in this way, you are radically different; you will never be the same again. When you are touched in this way you know and you say, "God, there is more of you, and I want more." It is the love of God that goes into the deepest recesses of the human soul. It is far more satisfying than any human relationship. Just as redeemed men and women are called sons of God; every redeemed man and woman is called the bride of Christ. What is fascinating is that redemptive history begins in the Garden of Eden with a wedding. It is a marriage that takes place between

Adam and Eve. Redemptive history concludes with a wedding, the marriage supper of the Lamb between the Bridegroom Christ and His bride the Church.

What is also fascinating is that Jesus began His ministry at a wedding. He was at the wedding in Cana performing a miracle where He turned water into wine. It is also fascinating that the first private instruction to His apostles were about Him, the Bridegroom, and them being friends of the bridegroom. He concluded His private instruction to the apostles with the instruction, "Make sure your oil lamps are filled lest you miss the bridegroom." Throughout this book we will be discussing God's eternal purpose about Christ the bridegroom and His bride, the church. Much of Scripture talks about this unique relationship between Christ and His eternal companion, His bride.

CHAPTER 1

God's Plan Unfolded

First, we are going to talk about God's eternal purpose.

Then God said, "Let Us make man in Our image, according to Our likeness; and let them rule over the fish of the sea and over the birds of the sky and over the cattle and over all the earth, and over every creeping thing that creeps on the earth." 27 God created man in His own image, in the image of God He created him; male and female He created them. 28 God blessed them; and God said to them, "Be fruitful and multiply, and fill the earth, and subdue it; and rule over the fish of the sea and over the birds of the sky and over every living thing that moves on the earth (Gen. 1:26–28).

There is approximately six thousand years of redemptive history. It all began with a wedding in the garden between Adam and Eve. It culminates as I've mentioned in a wedding feast, and that wedding is consummated with the bride of Christ ruling and reigning with Him in the Kingdom. In Revelation 2:26 Jesus himself says, "26He who overcomes, and he who keeps My deeds until the end, to him I will give authority over the nations." In Revelation 3:21, Jesus also says, "He who overcomes, I will grant to him to sit down with Me on My throne, as I also overcame and sat down with My Father on His throne." In Revelation 20:4–6, it says that the bride, the church will rule and reign with Christ for a thousand years. There will be a cooperation, a co-reigning in this new government called the Kingdom of God.

Right from the very beginning in eternity past, God had planned history with His Son having a bride, a companion that would co-reign with Him and enjoy Him forever. That is the eternal purpose of God in creating a bride for His Son. We see this picture taking place right here in the Garden of Eden. We are told that God had created a special race. It was the masterpiece of His created order. He created man in His own image and in His own likeness. Imagine just for a moment the shock that the angels had when God said that He was going to create a race that is far above them, a race that would be able to connect with Him on a heart level. The angels are masterful creatures, no doubt. They are brilliant creatures; they are powerful creatures. But they are creatures nonetheless who are servants only. Some have been rebellious servants who rejected God's authority. Satan and the demons rebelled and went their own way. However, the other angels, the good angels are nothing more than servants of God, sent forth to minister to those that are heirs of salvation (Heb. 1:14). This special creation of God, this masterpiece that God has created, is a race of people for whom God would prepare a bride. It would be out of a special people, a special relationship, an intimate friendship, companionship, affection, intimacy, and love beyond anything that any human can produce. It is a love fest that first and foremost is not sexual because it goes so much deeper than that. It goes to the deepest recesses of the human soul.

Then God did something even more amazing. He not only created this special race where He could walk with His creation in the garden, He had created a perfect son. A son named Adam that would fellowship with Him in the cool of the garden as they walked and enjoyed one another's company and fellowship. Adam enjoyed the fullness of the love of God and God had given him the right to govern over all His creation. Mankind was given the privilege of co-reigning with God over all of His domain. God had given Adam the privilege to share in His government. That is incredible! The right to co-reign with God. Yet you know the tragedy of the story. Eve got seduced by the tempter, a false lover, called the knowledge of good and evil.

Eve had a perfect relationship with her husband and she had a perfect relationship with God. Adam had a perfect relationship with God. The moment they rebelled against Him, shame, brokenness and condemnation entered the picture. From that moment on, human nature was darkened; they were alienated, separated, hostile to God and hostile to His ways. But God never stopped loving His creation. He never stopped loving His masterpiece, He never stopped loving the one to whom He would prepare a bride for. In the garden, God had created a willing bride for his son.

"The LORD God fashioned into a woman from the rib which He had taken from the man, and brought her to the man. The man said,

"This is now bone of my bones,
And flesh of my flesh;
She shall be called Woman,
Because she was taken out of Man."

For this reason, a man shall leave his father and his mother, and be joined to his wife; and they shall become one flesh. And the man and his wife were both naked and were not ashamed" (Gen. 2:22–25). This is such an amazing story because God had given Adam the right to govern His domain, to govern this new government. As Adam is naming the animals, as he is seeing them come two by two, both male and female when suddenly Adam realizes, "Hey, wait a minute, there is no help meet for me. I am not complete." You know the story, God said it is not good that man would be alone. In this passage, we see several prophetic pictures. The first picture is this: God put Adam to sleep and He took his rib out of his body. He fashioned a bride for His perfect son. What God did is that He made this beautiful creature who was called "Whoa, man!" LOL. Here is Papa God, creating this beautiful bride and introducing her to His perfect son, whose name is Adam. He is introducing his bride who is ready to embrace him. This image is still with us today. Whenever we have a wedding, it is the father that introduces his bride to the bridegroom. Then there is this consummation that takes place. It is an amazing love fest, intimate, affectionate, without brokenness, without shame. They are naked and unashamed. It is a complete, perfect, abiding love for one another.

Picture this, it is because of the fall, that God knew, in order to prepare this bride, He had to send a different Son, a perfect Son whose His name is Jesus. God allowed His perfect Son to become the betrothal price for this new bride. Jesus gave His life as the atoning sacrifice. The Father allowed His son to be brutalized beyond human recognition of a man to pay the redemptive price, the betrothal price for His bride. The worthy Son gave his life. As He was on the cross, He was pierced for our transgressions, He died. The words that the Scripture use for His death is that He fell asleep, just as Adam had fallen asleep. The picture is that just as God had taken the rib from Adam's side, the soldier thrust a spear in to the side of Jesus. It was through this redemptive act, the work on the cross that God is now fashioning a willing bride for a worthy Son. That's amazing. Despite all our flaws, despite all our insecurities, what is so amazing, is that the redemptive price Christ has paid on the cross has defeated Satan, sin, and death. Now the bride of Christ who is in the process of becoming, if you will, a virgin without spot or blemish. Or rather, has been declared a virgin without spot or blemish, and is now preparing herself to receive the bridegroom so that she can live with Him without shame.

There is another prophetic picture here. In Ephesians 5:25 it says, "For this reason a man shall leave his father and mother and be joined to his wife and they shall become one flesh." What is amazing is that this word *join* means to cleave. This word actually means to be bonded together as one. To be bonded as one gives you the picture of taking two boards, pressing them together with wood glue in the middle, pressing them as tight as possible until the wood dries. These two boards literally becomes one piece of wood. If you would to try to separate it, it would splinter apart. That is why Jesus said what God has joined together let no man separate. This marriage is not just an agreement, it is a covenant. Here we are told of the permanence of this covenant relationship between a husband and wife. It is talking about the permanence of the one flesh union. In other words, this covenant, if people were really to understand what covenant means, they would understand that no matter what offense takes place, they are under covenant. If you know you are under covenant and it's an unbreakable covenant, that means you have to fix it! The one who breaks the covenant is the one who refuses to fix it. They are the ones who abandon the relationship, they are the ones who refuse to reconcile and go their own way. The marriage covenant is an unbreakable covenant because there is a greater picture here. The apostle Paul in Ephesians 5:25 and following says, "Husbands love your wives as Christ loved the church and gave Himself up for her as a fragrant offering and sacrifice to God." A husband should care for his wife and nourish his wife, then Paul says, "For this reason a man shall leave his father and mother and be joined to his wife and the two will become one flesh. This mystery is great for I am speaking with reference to Christ and His church" (Eph. 5:31–32).

The word *mystery* is an interesting word. It means the secret plan of God that was hidden for ages past that is now being revealed. It's a great mystery. It's a mystery that was hidden in the Old Covenant, but it is a mystery that is being revealed to us. That wedding in the garden is more than a wedding of two people. It is a prophetic picture of the unbroken bond between Christ and His bride. It illustrates a love that is so deep for His people. An intimacy, a union, a communion that God so desperately wants for His children, the bride, for His worthy Son.

Our Papa in Heaven has sent His Son to pay that redemptive price, giving up His own perfect Son, who would pay not just the redemptive price for our Salvation, but also the betrothal price for our union and communion with Christ. Look at 2 Corinthians 11:2–3,

"For I am jealous for you with a godly jealousy; for I betrothed you to one husband, so that to Christ I might present you as a pure virgin. But I am afraid that, as the serpent deceived Eve by his craftiness, your minds will be led astray from the simplicity and purity of devotion to Christ." Focus on the word "betrothal." Many people call this the engagement period. In America, the engagement period is so much more different than the betrothal period in the early church and the Old Testament. The betrothal period really was a marital contract that could not be broken except by divorce or death. When you got betrothed you were considered to be legally married. Per Jewish law and tradition, you were given a pledge, this pledge was a signet ring. The signet ring indicated that you belonged to someone else. Hands off!

We know this to be true because Mary was betrothed to Joseph. Mary had an encounter with God, she had conceived the holy Son of God through the Spirit of God. She was found with child and Joseph being a righteous man was planning on divorcing her quietly so that this woman would not be embarrassed. An angel appeared before Joseph and said this child was conceived by the Holy Spirit. Therefore, Joseph didn't divorce Mary, He married her. He waited until the baby was born and he then consummated the marriage that had already taken place a year earlier.

God says He is jealous of you with a godly jealously because He betrothed you to one husband who is Jesus. So that to Christ, God may present you as a pure virgin. The marriage covenant is really nothing more than a prophetic picture of Christ and His bride. In this betrothal period, Jesus has given us a pledge. That pledge is the Holy Spirit. In Ephesians1:13 and following says this, now watch carefully … "In Him, you also, after listening to the message of truth, the gospel of your salvation—having also believed, you were sealed in Him with the Holy Spirit of promise, who is given as a *pledge* of our *inheritance*, with a view to the redemption of God's own possession, to the praise of His glory." That pledge is the sealing ministry of the Holy Spirit; it is the indwelling ministry of the Holy Spirit. In

Ephesians 4:30, it says you are sealed until the day of redemption. This seal cannot be broken.

The seal involves four things. First and foremost, it is a seal of ownership. When you are indwelt by the Holy Spirit of promise, God has put that deposit in you guaranteeing the redemption of the purchase possession. God is saying you belong to Me, I have paid the betrothal price for you. Secondly, it is a seal of identity. The Scriptures tell us in Romans 8:9 "If anyone does not have the Spirit of Christ, he does not belong to Christ." It is the Holy Spirit that marks us as a special child of God and as a future bride for His Son, the worthy Son, the Lord Jesus. It marks us as the child of God. Third, it is a seal of authority. The Holy Spirit in us gives us special authority to be God's representatives. Just like Jesus was a special representative on Earth. That is why Jesus said in Matthew 28:18, "All authority is given to me in heaven and on earth. Therefore go, and make disciples." It is the Holy Spirit in you that has given you the authority to speak in His name. Finally, it is a seal of security. No one and nothing can ever break that seal. It is safe, it is secure, and it guarantees our future redemption, because we belong to Him and He will not let His bride go. He says, "I am jealous of you with a godly jealously, for I betrothed you to one husband" (2 Cor. 11:2). Then he says, "But I am afraid that as the serpent deceived Eve by his craftiness your minds will be led astray from the simplicity and the purity of your devotion to Christ" (2 Cor. 11:3). He has given us an amazing prophetic picture, because Paul is referring all the way back to the garden, where the first marriage was instituted. He is saying Eve was deceived, because she followed a false lover, something grabbed her heart. Eve had it all; she lacked nothing. But the devil implied to her that God doesn't really love her. The devil in essence said, "Why don't you become like God knowing good and evil; there is something better out there for you, God is holding back." God doesn't really love you like He says he loves you. He doesn't love you like He declares, because He is holding back. Eve looks at the fruit and she sees that it looks good to the eyes, it looks like it's able to make one wise. She tastes it and it's good to the taste. It's nothing more than the lust of the flesh, the lust of the eyes, and the boastful pride of life. It is the same stinking lie the enemy tells us today. The enemy is after our hearts. He is trying to seduce our hearts from our first love. The enemy is jealous because he is not the masterpiece of God. He cannot connect with God on a heart level; he never could. So all he can do is thwart, seduce, and prevent the people of God from loving our bridegroom the way we should be loving our bridegroom.

It is a prophetic picture of Hosea and Gomer. Hosea was the prophet of God in the Old Testament. God said go select your wife, a harlot. Isn't that bizarre? I don't know about you, but I don't want to look over my shoulder and wonder what my wife is doing. God tells Hosea, "Get yourself a wife and it must be a harlot." Gomer, the wife of Hosea is an unfaithful woman. Hosea chases her time and time again. This demonstrates not only the prophetic picture that Israel is constantly playing the adulterous harlot, but it's a prophetic picture of even today of how often our hearts stray from the bridegroom and following after false lovers. You can call it whatever you want; it could be illicit relationships, or it could be pride, selfishness, busyness, apathy—the names can be infinite. No matter where you are in this spectrum, there is always more of God's intimacy. There is always more, there is always a deeper affectionate relationship with Him that we can experience. When you begin to experience this love, you are going to find that the stuff in this earth matters very little. You are going to realize that the burdens you carry are too heavy for you to carry, but there is someone greater than you that is willing to carry it. You begin to realize that your bridegroom is faithful who will supply all your needs according to His riches and glory. I am not just talking about financial needs or material needs. I am also talking about the needs in the deepest recesses of your heart.

When you connect with the love of God you cannot be anxious, because you are being filled with His perfect love and perfect love cast out all fear. This requires a passionate pursuit of God. When I was dating my wife Jamie, I was hot on her heels. I was chasing her all over the place. She is worth it. She is still worthy to chase; she's the babe. She is a beautiful woman. Our bridegroom is magnificent and He is looking for people whose heart is completely His. This is what He is looking for. "The eyes of the Lord go to and fro throughout the Earth looking for those whose heart is completely His" (2 Chron. 16:9). His eyes are on you right now. What does He see? I can't see what is in your heart and frankly I don't want to know. I have to deal with my own heart. But I can tell you this, if you seek God with all your heart, He will satisfy you with everything that your heart needs. He will satisfy you beyond your wildest imagination because His love goes so deep. His love is so satisfying, it is so refreshing, it is so beautiful, it is so intimate, so consuming, so magnificent that when you reach that place where you yell out, "God I want more!" That is when you know you just touched the surface.

I am at a place in my life where I am wrecked for Jesus. That is all I want. I want the fullness of the kingdom of God. I want to know Him; I want to know His ways. I can't get enough of God, because He just gives more and more and more. It doesn't mean that we are going to be perfect. It doesn't mean that we are not going to make mistakes. It doesn't mean that you are not going to experience conflict in your husband and wife relationships or your people to people relationships. But what it does mean is that when you encounter Him, you don't want to live in your brokenness. You will want to put it aside, and lay it on the cross. You will want to enjoy a deeper, abiding, love fest with him without any shame.

The bride of Christ is describing the kind of relationship we can have with Jesus. God is seeking willing lovers who would voluntarily seek His heart, surrender to Him, and love Him with all their heart, soul, mind and strength.

CHAPTER 2

An Overview

In this chapter, I will give you a summery overview of how God used an ancient Jewish wedding ceremony to illustrate the New Covenant truths concerning Christ the Bridegroom and His bride the church. Then as the chapters unfold, we will look at each aspect of this Jewish wedding ceremony in-depth and see how it relates to us as a church today.

If you read the Scripture from cover to cover you would discover that God teaches us in a variety of different ways. Sometimes God uses powerful word pictures, sometimes He uses symbols, sometimes He uses examples of people both good and bad. Sometimes God uses a direct word, an authoritative word, sometimes He uses examples from nature, like a tree planted by the rivers of water that will not cease to bear fruit.

God gives us an example of an ancient Jewish wedding ceremony that correlates with Christ, the Bridegroom, and His bride the church. It is absolutely amazing the correlation between the two. What was a mystery to the Jews, who by the way were called the bride of Yahweh, was revealed. The mystery was that both Jew and Gentile called the church, would be the bride of Christ. We are going to see an overview of this plan unfold throughout the rest of this chapter and then we will look deeper into each aspect of this ceremony in the following chapters.

The first step in the process of a wedding ceremony in the Old Testament is called the Shiddukhin. This refers to the arrangements prior to betrothal. In Genesis 24:1–4 we see Abraham is going to take responsibility to arrange a marriage for his son. He is going to define the marital contract and look for a willing bride for his son. "Now Abraham was old, advanced in age; and the Lord had blessed Abraham in every way. ²Abraham said to his servant, the oldest of his household, who had charge of all that he owned, 'Please place your hand under my thigh, ³and I will make you swear by the Lord, the God of heaven and the God of earth, that you shall not take a wife for my son from the daughters of the Canaanites, among whom I live, ⁴but you will go to my country and to my relatives, and take a wife for my son Isaac.'" Here Abraham is now older. If you remember he had a son Isaac when he was old in age, and he recognizes now that his son is of the age to be married. He recognizes his responsibility as a father to arrange a marriage for his son. What Abraham does, is that he selects his oldest, most trusted servant. This servant was going to act as a matchmaker for his son. Abraham makes the servant take a vow. The vow is do not, in the name of the Lord Yahweh, take a wife for my son from among the pagan people, especially from the Canaanites. But rather go to my relatives, my country men, go to God's people and select a willing bride for my son. That bride had to be a willing bride; he wasn't going to just kidnap a woman. The servant was very concerned about this, so he asks Abraham, 'What if she says no?' This was a legitimate concern for the servant. Abraham replied, 'If she says no, you are free from your obligation.'" She must be a willing bride.

Several things happened here. The father Abraham is responsible to find the bride. He uses a mediator, a matchmaker, his servant to set up this marital contract. He is going to look for among God's people a willing bride for his son. I've mentioned how God, even before the foundations of the world, He created a special race of people. Out of that race, He would prepare a bride for His Son. In the same way, Scripture says in Ephesians 1:3–4 that we are chosen in Him before the foundations of the world. In love, He predestined us, He adopted us as sons through Jesus Christ to Himself according to the good pleasure of His glory. God not only planned a bride for His son, but He planned a willing bride for His son. This willing bride that He planned is you and I. Even before the foundations of the world, God has chosen and predestined us to become that willing bride and He used a match maker. That matchmaker is the Holy Spirit. That matchmaker, the Holy Spirit is the one that convicts us of sin, that we were alienated from God, that we were separated from God, that we were hostile towards God and His ways. That we were children of wrath. It was the Holy Spirit that began to woo us. In fact, it was Jesus Himself that said no one can come to the Father unless the Holy Spirit draws him and I will raise him up on that last day (John 6:44). It was the Holy Spirit that brought us to a place of repentance, recognizing that apart from God we are lost. The Scriptures say it is the kindness of God that bring us to repentance (Rom. 2:4). It was the Holy Spirit that imparted faith to us that we could respond willingly to His kindness. It says in Ephesians 2:8–9, "For by grace you are saved through faith and this is not of yourselves." Even the response we had towards God is because of the faith God imparted through the Holy Spirit. It is a gift of God not a result of works lest any man should boast. It is the Holy Spirit that is the matchmaker that brought us to that place where we said yes to Jesus Christ. Where we willingly and voluntarily surrendered to Him, where we willing and voluntarily said, "Lord, here is my life I give it to you, I surrender and I choose to love you and follow you." It was our Heavenly Father who arranged that marriage, a willing bride for His Worthy Son. You are that willing bride."

The second part of this process is called the ketubah; this is the marriage contract itself. "When Abraham's servant heard their words, he bowed himself to the ground before the Lord. The servant brought out articles of silver and articles of gold, and garments, and gave them to Rebekah; he also gave precious things to her brother and to her mother" (Gen. 24:52–53). Abraham's servant received instructions from Abraham and he goes off on this journey. We know he meets Rebekah at the well. Rebekah had been the one he prayed for and this connection is made and he goes to her family. What this man is going to do is arrange a contract. The word *ketubah* literally means "written." This refers to the plan, the proposal and the condition of this marital contract. In this marital contract, the groom promises to love the bride, he promises to protect her, provide for her, care for her. In this contract, the groom not only promises to love her but he agrees to a bridal price. The contract also states what the bride will do. The bride will be faithful to her groom. She will be faithful to love him and to wait for him. The groom during the betrothal period has to go away and prepare a home for her. During this period, the bride promises to wait for her husband, she promises to be faithful to him. She promises to be fully devoted to him alone. This martial contract in the New Covenant spells out what the bridal price will be for Christ's bride. It is also a promise that Christ the bridegroom will love His bride, that He will provide for His bride that He will care for His bride, that He will be fully devoted to His bride. He is going to provide for her, protect her, love her, to care for her. The bride will be fully loved and accepted by the bridegroom. The contract also stipulates what the bride will do. In Abraham's case, the bride must pay the dowry. All that she has and all that she owns belongs to him and she promises to love him. In the same way, the moment that we willingly surrender to Christ, the moment we willingly trusted Him as our Savior and Lord, all that we are, all that we have and all that we ever hope to be, belongs to Him. "Or do you not know that your body is a temple of the Holy Spirit who is in you, whom you have from God, and that you are not your own? [20]For you have been bought with a price: therefore glorify God in your body" (1 Cor. 6:19–20). In this contract it is the bride that says I am willing to love you, serve you, and follow you. I am willing to surrender and yield to you as my leader and as my love.

The third process is the Mohar, the bridal payment, see again Genesis 24:52–53. The servant went and negotiated a bridal price.

In this contract, the bridal price was fully spelled out and the match-maker agreed to this bridal price. He then brought out some of the gold and some of the garments he had prepared for this negotiated price. It is the payment for the betrothal.

The bridal price that Jesus our bridegroom paid, was the full price that our redemption demanded and that was the giving of His life as an atoning sacrifice for our sin. "Knowing that you were not redeemed with perishable things like silver or gold or from your futile way of life inherited from your forefathers, but with precious blood, as of a lamb unblemished and spotless, the blood of Christ" (1 Pet. 1:18–19). When Jesus Christ was at Calvary, when He was whipped, beaten and brutally murdered on the cross and when he expelled His last breath. "He said, it is finished," the price has been paid in full. Jesus paid the Mohar, the bridal payment for His bride, you, and I.

The next process in this relationship is the Mikveh, the ritual immersion. What is fascinating is that even though it is not spelled out in Scripture and not in the contract itself, this was a very import-ant custom in an ancient Jewish wedding and it still is. The Mikveh in the Old Covenant is the baptism in the New Covenant. It was cus-tomary for both the groom and the bride to go through the Mikveh, a ritual immersion, or ritual cleansing. In this cleansing the groom was saying to His bride, "I am set apart for you and you alone. I am pure, holy, and devoted to you." The bride also went through the Mikveh. She was immersed in water and also declared, "I am holy, I am pure. I am set apart for you and you alone." This was vitally important. It demonstrated that the groom was pure and the bride was a pure virgin, and they were coming together in a holy covenant of marriage in a pure way, completely set apart for one another.

Then Jesus arrived from Galilee at the Jordan coming to John, to be baptized by him. But John tried to prevent Him, saying, "I have need to be baptized by You, and do You come to me?" But Jesus answering said to him, "Permit it at this time; for in this way it is fitting for us to fulfill all righteousness." Then he permitted Him (Matt. 3:13–15).

Do you know why John was confused? John was confused because he was practicing a baptism of repentance. John had said to the Pharisees, "Repent and be baptized for the remission of sins." Now Jesus comes along and he knows that Jesus is the sinless lamb of God who came to take away the sin of the world. He saw that Jesus was Messiah, and that Jesus did not need a baptism of repentance. In essence, John is asking, "Why are you here, I need to be baptized by you?" John didn't understand that Jesus wasn't doing a baptism of repentance. Jesus was doing the Mikveh. When Jesus was baptized to fulfill all righteousness, Jesus was saying, "I am holy, I am set apart for my bride. I am prepared for you, I am sept apart for you and you alone." Jesus is preparing Himself for His bride, the church. Look at what Jesus says in Matthew 28:18–20, "All authority in heaven and earth has been given to me, therefore, go make disciples of all nations baptizing them in the name of the Father, the Son, and the Holy Spirit teaching them to obey everything I have commanded you and lo I am with you always even until the end of the age."

Do you realize that the New Covenant baptism is not the baptism of repentance like John's. The reason is because faith and repentance have already occurred, and we entered into a covenant relationship with God. Baptism in the New Covenant is the fulfillment of the Mikveh. It is the bride of Christ saying, "I am set apart solely for you, I am holy. I am redeemed from the world system. I've been delivered from the kingdom of darkness. I have been brought with a price, and therefore Lord Jesus, I am your bride and I will follow you." It is the Mikveh. It is so important in the New Covenant. When we are baptized, it is not just being dipped in water, it is a powerful symbol that you and I have been set apart from the kingdom of darkness and set apart for Christ and Him alone.

The next process is the Eyrusin; this is the betrothal period. In the betrothal ceremony both the bride and groom drink a cup of blessing. This is a cup of wine that is shared by both the bride and the groom. "For I am jealous for you with a godly jealousy; for I betrothed you to one husband, so that to Christ I might present you as a pure virgin" (2 Cor. 11:2). Now, Jesus at the last supper as He took the cup and said, "I will not drink of the fruit of the wine until I come into my kingdom." Jesus will not drink the cup of wine until the marriage supper of the Lamb.

Next in the betrothal period, once they take part in this cup of blessing, the groom gives a pledge, usually a ring and then the groom leaves for about a year. During that year, he is planning and preparing a home for his bride. He usually goes back to his father's home. He either builds an addition to the home or builds a separate house in a complex or on a farm, whatever their finances can afford. During this time, the bride has declared and promised to wait for her bridegroom. She promises to be alert and to be faithful to him and him alone. She has been given a signet ring that declares she belongs to someone and is taken already, that she is married already.

The betrothal is more than just an engagement; it is a legally binding contract of which the only way to get out of it is through a divorce or death. We know this because when Joseph found out Mary was with child, he was going to divorce her quietly thinking she was unfaithful. When he found out that the baby was conceived through the Holy Spirit, he legally married her but did not consummate the marriage until after the baby was born. As Jesus was preparing to pay the bridal price for our redemption and our betrothal, he drank the last cup of wine and it was the cup of blessing. Then Jesus gave us a pledge. It's not the signet ring; it was something far greater, it is the sealing ministry of the Holy Spirit. Remember what Ephesians 1:13–14 says, "In Him, you also, after listening to the message of truth, the gospel of your salvation—having also believed, you were sealed in Him with the Holy Spirit of promise who is *given as a pledge* of our inheritance, with a view to the redemption of God's own possession, to the praise of His glory." As discussed, this pledge is the sealing ministry of the Holy Spirit.

The betrothal was approximately nine months to a year in the Old Covenant. The bride did not know when the exact day would come, but she knew it would be soon. The closer it came to a year's time, she would be waiting, expecting, looking, and longing for the bridegroom to come. Scripture tells us in the Matthew 24, "That no man knows the day or the hour the bridegroom returns but you should know the season. The bride of Christ should be waiting expectantly, fully prepared for the bridegroom."

The next process is the Matan, which is the bridal gift. Abraham had given his servant a whole lot of stuff. He had given him a lot of silver, gold, and a lot of garments. It was not just to pay the bridal price. Once the betrothal was given and the pledge was made then he gave gifts. Let me suggest to you that after the bridal price was paid, then Abraham's servant gave extravagant gifts. It is the same in the New Covenant. But to each one of us grace was given according to the measure of Christ's gift. Therefore it says,

> *"When He ascended on high,*
> *He led captive a host of captives,*
> *And He gave gifts to men" (Ephesians 4:7–8).*

There are two kinds of gifts that are mentioned here in the Scriptures; there are grace gifts or what I would call redemptive gifts that every believer receives at salvation. These redemptive gifts are the gift of helps, the gift of serving, the gift of giving, the gift of leadership, the gift of administration. There are all kinds of redemptive gifts that every believer gets the moment of conversion. He not only purchased and gave redemptive gifts but He also purchased *Charismata* gifts. "When he ascended on high, He led captive a host of captives and he gave Charismata to men." From the word *charismata* we also get the word spirituals. These are spiritual gifts. We see these spiritual gifts unfolded at Pentecost. We see them listed in the nine gifts of the Holy Spirit in 1 Corinthians 12 and 14, the gifts of power, faith, healing, miracles. The gifts of prophecy, tongues, interpretation of tongues, the gift of words of wisdom and words of knowledge. These gifts are expressions of love that Jesus Christ gave to His church. Just as Abraham's servant gave gifts to remind the bride that these gifts are for you and they are to be used and enjoyed. In the body of Christ, the gifts of the Holy Spirit have been given to us to use and enjoy and build up the body of Christ so that we become a mature measure of the stature of Christ.

The next process is the Nissuin, the marriage itself. When the bridegroom went through the betrothal ceremony, they drank from the cup, he gave her the ring, gave her the gifts and then went back to his father's house. During this whole year, he is building his bride a home and she is waiting expectantly for his return. She doesn't know the hour or the day, but she is waiting and watching. The word Nissuin means to carry or snatch. The bride is waiting for the bridegroom to snatch her away and carry her off to her new home. She's waiting for her bridegroom to come. She's waiting for him; she's anticipating him. She gets snatched up and he brings her to the home in a processional. One of the guests of this ceremony is blowing a shofar; it's a celebration. They get to the home; he takes her to the marriage chamber in the new home and then the guests celebrate at the marriage feast. This marriage feast is not just a good meal and a good celebration of dancing. It is seven full days of feasting on good food, music, dancing, and joyful celebration.

The symbolism is really amazing. Here we are in the final days of redemption. I believe we are in the season of Christ's return. Jesus will soon snatch His bride the church in what we often describe as the Rapture of the church (1 Th. 4:13–18). In Matthew 25, Jesus teaches the parable of the ten virgins. There are some that know the bridegroom is coming and they are filling their lamps with oil in preparation. There are some that are saying, "Well, I have time, I can do whatever I want". They are going to miss the bridegroom. The bridegroom is coming and the bride must be prepared. The bridegroom (Jesus) is immediately going to snatch her up and carry His bride to His home, the home that He has prepared. What takes place at this moment is that they will drink the ceremonial cup of blessing, the cup that Jesus said, "I will not drink until I come into my kingdom." At this moment Jesus and His bride the church drink this cup and then they feast. I believe the seven days represented in the Jewish marital ceremony is really a correlation with the seven years of the tribulation period, culminating with the marriage super of the Lamb. After this marriage takes place and the seven days are complete, the husband and wife in the Old Covenant are joined together as one and they co-reign together in their household. In the same way, in the marriage supper of the lamb, after this grand celebration, Jesus returns with His bride to establish a kingdom in which the bride now co-reigns. Jesus says in Revelation 2:26, "to the one who over comes I will grant him authority over the nations." In Revelation 3:21, Jesus says, "To him that over comes I will grant him authority to sit on my throne." For the rest of eternity, the bride and the bridegroom will be consummated as one and will join in a deep union and communion with Him forever. Again, it's not a sexual union; you must understand that. It is not a union of shame or guilt or fear or insecurity. It is a union of the deepest, intimate communion that man can ever experience. It is the love of God that goes beyond all comprehension.

So where does this leave us right now? It leaves us as the bride waiting for her bridegroom. Don't follow false lovers. There are a lot of false lovers. The enemy is always trying to steal your heart. You have been betrothed to one husband and that is Christ. He paid the bridal price for you. He satisfied the righteous requirement that your sin demanded so that you can have that covenant relationship with Him, a covenant that is unbreakable. It is important for us to understand that the whole purpose of the prophecy of Hosea, when Hosea married Gomer, that the devil is always trying to make us into a harlot. The enemy is always trying to seduce our heart so that we would be unfaithful to our husband, who is Christ. It is important for us understand 1 John 3:2: "Beloved, now we are children of God, and it has not appeared as yet what we will be. We know that when He appears, we will be like Him, because we will see Him just as He is. ³And *everyone* who has this hope fixed on Him purifies himself, just as He is pure." It's all about the heart. That's the message of the bridegroom to the bride. He wants your heart. He wants His bride to be fully, wholly, devoted to the bridegroom. What if He showed up today? Scripture says the rapture of His church is imminent. "¹⁶For the Lord Himself will descend from heaven with a shout, with the voice of the archangel and with the trumpet of God, and the dead in Christ will rise first. Then we who are alive and remain will be caught up together with them in the clouds to meet the Lord in the air, and so we shall always be with the Lord. Therefore comfort one another with these words" (1 Th. 4:16–18). Be prepared. Have you trimmed your oil lamps? Is your heart fully devoted to Him? Remember the passage in Revelation where Jesus was speaking to the Ephesians. Jesus tells them, I know your works, you've done a great job, you have exposed false teachers, you have done all these great things but one thing I have against you, you left your first love. You didn't lose it, you left it. I believe we are in a generation where God is calling His bride to prepare for the bridegroom. We are that generation, I believe, will experience the return of Christ. Are you ready for His return?

CHAPTER 3

The Shidukhin: Arrangements Preliminary to Betrothal

There were several mysteries in the Old Testament that are now revealed in the New Testament. For instance, Christ in you the hope of glory. In the Old Covenant, the Holy Spirit came and went. The Holy Spirit would empower a believer for a specific act of service or for a season and then the Holy Spirit would leave. In the New Covenant, the moment you trust Christ you are indwelt by the Holy Spirit of promise; you are sealed until the day of redemption and you are empowered by God to do what God has called us to do. God says, "I will never leave you nor forsake you." That was a mystery in the Old Covenant that was revealed in the new. Another mystery is that Jew and Gentile will be one new man, we will be one in Christ. Gentiles today are no longer strangers to the covenant of promise; they are no longer without God or without hope in the world, but now in Christ Jesus we who were far off have been made near by the blood of Christ (Eph. 2:12–13). That means that every believer today, Jew and Gentile, have the same covenantal promises of God. We have the same access to God, which is an incredible promise, but it was hidden in the past. The believers in the Old Covenant believed that the Gentiles were nothing more than a curse, separate from God without hope, but now we are one in Christ. The snatching up of the church which is called the rapture, was also hidden in the Old Covenant. Paul says in 1 Corinthians 15:51, "Behold I tell you a mystery that we will not all sleep but we will be all changed in a twinkling of the eye the dead in Christ shall rise." The bride of Christ was also hidden. In Ephesians 5, Paul says, "Husbands love your wives as Christ loved the church and gave Himself up for her as a fragrant offering and a sacrifice to God." Just a few verses later it says, "This is a profound mystery, but I am speaking in reference to Christ and His church." That mystery is that the bride of Christ is the church. That one day we are going to enjoy an intimate union and communion with Christ forever. Again, it is important for you to know that this is not a sexual union but rather a spiritual union. This union is about intimacy. An intimacy far greater than any human intimacy. Unfortunately today, there are so many believers who treat their bridegroom Jesus as nothing more than an acquaintance. The purpose of Christ and the bridegroom is that we would enjoy a deep, intimate, union, and communion with Him now and forevermore. The moment you trusted Christ, your eternity began that moment. You are one with Him at that moment. Someday that union will be consummated in the kingdom of God when your faith will be made sight, but for now, we are in a pursuit of intimacy as the bride pursuing Jesus our bridegroom.

We have spoken about God's eternal purpose; that God would choose an acceptable bride for His worthy Son. Then we touched on how God often times teaches in symbols and word pictures and sometimes in examples of people both good and bad. God uses a powerful picture of the ancient Jewish custom of marriage to illustrate the fullness of Christ and His bride. All parts of the marriage were summarized in the past, now I am going to go into more detail.

The Shiddukhin is the arrangement prior to the betrothal period. The passage referring to Abraham is probably the greatest example of the Shiddukhin (see Gen. 24:1–4). By this time, Abraham was old and advanced in years. In fact, he was old when he had Isaac so you can imagine how much older he is even at this point. He recognizes his responsibility as a father to make an arrangement of a marriage for his son. In the Old Covenant, according to Jewish tradition, marriages were arranged. That is not so today. Today you look for a spouse, you hope that you connect, and when you do, you get married. But not in the Old Covenant, it was the father's responsibility to find an acceptable wife for his son. Abraham understands that responsibility. He is the Patriarch; he is papa, and he has enlisted his most trusted servant for the task. He tells his trusted servant, his matchmaker, not to go to the ungodly land of the Canaanities. Instead, Abraham commanded his servant to go to his relatives, to the people of faith and take a wife for his son. If you remember, the servant was somewhat concerned and confused and wondered, "What if she says no, they don't even know me." Then Abraham said that he would release him this task, why? Because she must be willing.

What is interesting is that Abraham enlisted his servant to become that matchmaker for his son. He gave him that responsibility to choose an acceptable bride for his son. The servant took gold and silver and all kinds of articles of clothing for the bride price and gifts to be given to the family. He goes to this land and sees this beautiful woman. He doesn't know that this is Rebekah and this is Abraham's relative. The servant prays, "God, if this is the one, have that woman draw water from the well." Sure enough, God answers, she draws water, and he knows instantly that he has favor from the Lord. He goes to the household, he brings back Rebekah, and she becomes Isaac's bride.

It's important to understand that this is a prophetic picture of Christ and the bride. You're going to find this amazing because just as it was Abraham's responsibility to find a bride for his son, so it is also Papa God's responsibility to find an acceptable bride for His Son. It is Father God choosing a bride for His son. "For as a young man marries a virgin, so your builder will marry you; and as a bridegroom rejoices over the bride, so your God will rejoice over you" (Isaiah

62:5). Here is a prophetic picture if you will, God is saying one day the builder, and who is the builder? Christ; upon this rock, I will build this church. Who is the rock, Christ, it's not Peter, it's Christ. Peter is a stone, that's all he is, he is a little stone, but Christ is the rock whom the church is built upon.

"As a bridegroom rejoices over the bride so God *rejoices* over you." Did you know God rejoices over you, did you know he sings and dances over you? Do you know how delighted he is with you? We will see this further as we move along. "Peter, an apostle of Jesus Christ, to those who reside as aliens, scattered throughout Pontus, Galatia, Cappadocia, Asia and Bithynia, who are chosen according to the foreknowledge of God the father, by the sanctifying work of the Spirit, to obey Jesus Christ and be sprinkled with His blood" (1 Peter 1:1–2). This Scripture shows all three persons of the Godhead participating in our salvation. Notice the roll of Papa God. The roll of Papa God is this, "*Who are chosen according to the foreknowledge of God the father.*" Papa God chose you to be a bride for His Son. Now there are those that may say, "Well, God foreknew those that would pick Him," but that is seriously wrong, that is error. We are told in Ephesians 1:3 that we are chosen in Him before the foundations of the earth. I don't know about you, but I wasn't around before the foundations of the earth, I wasn't even a sparkle in my mother's eye. We were chosen in Him before the foundations of the earth. In other words, Father God looked into eternity future to see those He foreknew who He would choose as an acceptable bride for His worthy Son. Now let's look at the second person of the trinity, "*by the sanctifying work of the Spirit.*" Friends, just as Abraham picked his trusted friend, the matchmaker for his son, God the Father sends the Holy Spirit as the matchmaker for His Son. He is the one who uses the Holy Spirit to bring us into that relationship with the Lord Jesus Christ.

Finally, we see Jesus Christ Himself; He is the one who paid the Mohar, the bride price. He is the one that sprinkled and shed His blood to satisfy our sin debt in full. Let's look at Roman's 9. I know that some of you really struggle with this issue of choosing. You may say, "I thought that you had to be willing." Yes, you do; we will get to that. What does it mean to be chosen by God? You know that the bride of Christ was a mystery in the Old Covenant that is being revealed in the New Covenant, but not God's choosing. That has never been a mystery. Did you know God chose Adam and Eve? He chose to make them, He chose to create them. They didn't just pop up; they didn't just evolve from an amoeba. He chose specifically to create them. After they rebelled against God what did they do? Did they run to God? No, they chose to hide. They chose the first religion of the world by covering their nakedness and shame with figs leaves. False religion is nothing more than trying to cover up your own sin. As they hid themselves from God, who did the chasing? God. God chased them down. "Where are you Adam?" God knew where he was; He chased him down. God sacrificed the animals to cover their guilt, shame as well as their naked bodies. It is a perfect picture of redemption and the atonement of Christ.

Abram was hanging out with the Chaldees. Abram was just being Abram when all of a sudden God shows up and says, "Hey, I want you to go to a land you do not know of and I will give you land, seed, and blessing." Abram just replied, "Okay, here I go." But who did the choosing? It was God. In every circumstance, if you study the Scriptures, God happens to show up in human history and transforms people by a word He speaks, in calling them to Himself. The calling of God was never a mystery in the Old Testament; in fact, it was a reality. We have an illustration that the apostle Paul is giving to us in Romans 9:11–14. "For though the twins were not yet born and had not done anything good or bad, so that God's purpose according to His choice would stand, not because of works but because of Him who calls, it was said to her, "The older will serve the younger." Just as it is written, "Jacob I loved, but Esau I hated. What shall we say then? There is no injustice with God, is there? May it never be! For He says to Moses, 'I will have mercy on whom I have mercy, and I will have compassion on whom I have compassion.'" I am sure that 90 percent of you reading this are saying, "I hate that passage of Scripture." I know because I was one of them. We think it's not fair. Part of it is because we don't understand the language at times. When we think of God's love for mankind, we think about the passage "God so loved the world that He gave His only begotten son that whosoever believe in Him shall not perish but have everlasting life" (John 3:16). God loves everyone, however, in a passage like this, the writer Paul is using language, but not in the same sense that we understand it. The context determines the meaning of the word. Paul is not speaking of human emotion at this point. He is saying that God had chosen Jacob but Esau he avoided. It was not based on what they did or did not do. It was not because Jacob was any better. The name Jacob means deceiver. Jacob lived in full compliance to his name. He was just as wicked as Esau who sold his birthright for a meal.

In Jewish culture, it was customary for the older child to receive the birth-right blessing. This meant they would get two-thirds of the inheritance. They would become the Patriarch when the father passed away. They will have all the influence, most of the wealth and blessed beyond measure. The younger siblings would serve him. Yet in this passage of Scripture, the older will serve the younger. It was prophesized in that moment that Jacob would receive the birthright. What is that birth right? It is faith. By grace you are saved through faith, that is the birthright. It was God who chose the younger to be served by the older. It was God who chose Jacob, not because he was any better, and God's choice will stand. It is God that always does the choosing.

I still didn't answer the question. If God does the choosing, how is it we have to be willing if we can't possibly be willing? Let's look at Ephesians 2:1–3: "As for you, you were dead in your transgressions and sins, in which you used to live when you followed the ways of this world and of the ruler of the kingdom of the air, the spirit who is now at work in those who are disobedient. All of us also lived among them at one time, gratifying the cravings of our flesh and following its desires and thoughts. Like the rest, we were by nature deserving of wrath." Let me ask you a question. If we are born dead in sin, then that means that we are a spiritual corpse. Did you ever see a corpse respond? Have you ever been to a funeral? Have you ever seen a dead person? Do they respond? Dead is dead. Scripture says we were dead in our sins. Paul is not talking about physical death; he is talking about spiritual death. The word dead here means "to be separated and alienated from God." There was nothing in us that could possibly say, "Oh, I get it." We are not the ones chasing God, He is chasing us. How do we get from the point of being dead in sin and alienated from God, to the point where we are willing to say yes to God? The matchmaker, the Holy Spirit. "No one can come to me *unless the Father who sent me draws them,* and I will raise them up at the last day" (John 6:44). That's the Holy Spirit's job. God the Father is sending out the Holy Spirit, the matchmaker to His people, whom He has chosen before the foundations of the world. He is wooing you and convicting you. "And He, when He comes, will convict the world concerning sin and righteousness and judgment; concerning sin, because they do not believe in Me; and concerning righteousness, because I go to the Father and you no longer see Me; and concerning judgment, because the ruler of this world has been judged" (John 16:8–11). The Holy Spirit convicts us in three areas. He convicts us of sin. What is sin? Sin is ultimately rebellion and hostility against God and His ways. When the Holy Spirit begins to speak into the deadness of our hearts, then all of a sudden, instead of thinking we are good we recognize we are sinful and we need a Savior. As He continues to convict and woo us He begins to enlighten us as to who Christ is. The Holy Spirit begins to illuminate who Christ is and why He came. Jesus is the God man that came to satisfy our sin debt. The Holy Spirit convicts of us of judgment. It is the Holy Spirit that begins to awaken our hearts to the reality that apart from Christ we are eternally lost. He is the matchmaker. If the Holy Spirit didn't move in our heart we would all reject God and do whatever we wanted to do. We would shake our fist in defiance and say, "I want to do what I want to do *because I am god.*" Just as it was in the Garden of Eden, when the snake said to Eve, "You can be like God, knowing good and evil." It is the Holy Spirit that is the matchmaker. Even the faith that we believe is a gift from God. "For it is by grace you have been saved, through faith—*and this is not from yourselves*, it is the gift of God—not by works, so that no one can boast" (Eph. 2:8–9).

We know salvation is a gift of God but often times people misinterpret this verse (Ephesians 2:8–9). This verse is not speaking of salvation as a gift of God. This verse is saying that the very faith we exercise is the gift of God; it does not come from any human desire or merit. Faith is the impartation of the Holy Spirit, the manifestation of the matchmaker who brings us to a place where we are to understand our sinfulness, understand we are separated from God and understand who Christ is and why He came. Then in a moment, through the Holy Spirit's work in us, repentance, and faith is awakened in our hearts and we respond to God by saying, "Yes, Lord, I repent of my sins and accept Jesus as my Lord and Savior!" When you really come to understand that God is the one moving from the beginning in our salvation to the very consummation of it; you cannot help but to be thankful. Apart from His work in our lives, we would be like Esau. He would have left us to determine our own destiny. You may wonder why is this important. The book of Romans is the book about justification by faith in Christ alone; it is about sanctification. It is about God taking a sinful person who is apart from God, who is hostile to God and bringing him to faith in Christ and then empowering the believer to live for Him. Chapters 1 all the way to chapter 11 is all about God's work in saving us. Then in chapter 12 verse 1, it says, "I urge you, brothers and sisters, in view of God's mercy, to offer your bodies as a living sacrifice, holy and pleasing to God—this is your true and proper worship." When you fully understand the work of God through the Father calling you before the foundations of the world, the Holy Spirit wooing you and convicting you, and imparting to you faith and repentance, and that the Lord Jesus paid the Mohar, the bride price, satisfied your sin debt in full; you then realize, "Wow, God you did that for me?" You then come to grips with the reality that you are special. You are not insignificant. You are not some blip on the screen, you are not some amoeba that somehow evolved, you are not what the world says you are as it tries to put you into its mold. You are a child of God who is special and has been set apart, who has been justified, sanctified, who is empowered by the Holy Spirit and set apart for Him. That is why when you get to Romans chapter 12 and Paul says, "Therefore, be fervent in your spirit." The word *fervent* means "be zealous."

Over the years, I have seen some of the most apathetic people in my life. Have you seen people that can't even open their lips because there is no praise in their hearts toward God? It is because they don't know who He is, they don't understand what He has done, they don't understand the magnificence of who He has made you to be. When you understand who God is and what He has done for you, when you understand the high and exalted position He has put you in, that you are seated in heavenly places with Christ. When you realize this, you cannot help but to be zealous for Him. You can't! That is why Scripture says, "Be fervent in your spirit. Be fervent in your love for one another. Be fervent in your job, doing the work of God in your workplace. Be fervent in your community by representing Him with kindness and grace. Be fervent in your service to the Lord. Be fervent in your worship." Apathy has no part in the kingdom of God; it just doesn't. Apathy does not cut it. God has called us to be zealous, to be fervent in our love for him and in our love for one another. That is why this matters. When you understand your identity in Christ and all that He has done for you, how He has awakened you and you realize that at one time you were an object of wrath. When you realize that if the Holy Spirit did not move in your heart and if God said "I will release you to your own destiny which you have determined," you would be in hell forever. You can't help but be thankful. Hell is a scary place. You may then ask the question, why do we evangelize? That's a question I get asked all the time. Do you know why we evangelize? It's because we don't know who He has chosen. But here is what I have found, God is glorified when a person rejects Him and God is glorified when a person accepts Him. He is glorified when people reject Him because His is a Holy God, a just God and He will punish sin and He will be glorified through that. He will demonstrate His holiness. The second reason we evangelize is because He commands us to. Evangelism is our work, not the angels. Although I do not know who will respond to the gospel, I do know some will.

When someone comes to Christ, when they come to repentance and they listen to the Holy Spirit prompting them and bringing them and awakening them. They are responding by faith and He is glorified through that because the work of the cross is now being completed in that believer's life. Now that person is being released into a new identity as a child of God as well as a new destiny. God is glorified through this. It is essential that we as believers understand that we are part of a different kingdom.

CHAPTER 4

The Ketubah,
The Marriage Covenant and
The Mohar, The Bridal Payment

A s we continue to study the bride of Christ, it is important to remember that this is not a sexual relationship but a deeper, intimate relationship. Jesus is the lover of our souls. It's important that we know God is calling us into a deep, intimate relationship with Him. Tragically, what I have discovered is that there are so many believers that treat their relationship with God as if He were just an acquaintance. The purpose of this book is to cause us to open wide our heart to receive His intimate love and friendship. That is the purpose of the whole bridal covenant between Christ and His bride.

When we look at Scripture, the Old Covenant, when we look at Genesis all the way to Malachi, these Scriptures represent Christ. What we see are prophetic pictures that the New Covenant begins to highlight and reveal. As we look at the Bride of Christ, it was a profound mystery as we had discussed before that was hidden in the Old Covenant but is released in the new. When we look at the bride of Christ, we can see prophetic pictures that are being revealed.

Adam and Eve are a prophetic picture of Christ and His bride, the church. Adam was the holy, sinless son of God. Jesus is called the second Adam, the Holy, sinless, Son of God. Eve is the prophetic picture of the bride of Christ. She was created, chosen, and set apart by God. She was holy, sinless, without spot or blemish. She was naked with her husband and completely without shame. This is the picture of the bride of Christ. Because of the blood of the Lamb, we are washed and cleansed, and we can walk with Him in intimacy without shame.

Consider Rebekah, she is another prophetic picture of the bride of Christ in complete submission and yieldedness to the Holy Spirit. It was Abraham who sent his servant, the matchmaker who was led by God. He went to the land where Abraham's family lived. It was there that he called out for God to lead him. God reveals to Abraham's servant that Rebekah is *the one*. Rebekah, then in complete submission allowed this person she has never met before, to take her where Abraham lived and became Isaac's bride. This is the trust and submission that represents the bride of Christ in complete yieldedness and submission to the Holy Spirit as He leads us and guides us to the place that we should go.

Queen Esther is another prophetic picture of the bride of Christ engaging in spiritual warfare. The wicked Haman had set up the Jewish people to be destroyed. Queen Esther, under the guidance of Mordecai, went boldly into the king's chamber even at the expense of her life. She exposed Haman's wicked plans and consequently he was hung on the gallows and the people of Israel were restored. This is a prophetic picture of the bride of Christ who wrestles not against flesh and blood but against principalities, powers, against rulers of this dark world, and spirits of wickedness in the heavenly places (Eph. 6:12).

Ruth is the prophetic picture of the Gentile bride who was brought from a place of hopelessness to exalted glory. Boaz, the kinsman redeemer, paid the bridal price for her, taking her from a place of desperation to an exalted place. In the same way, Gentiles who were without hope, strangers to the covenant of promise, without God in the world, completely hopeless and helpless; God has rescued them, Christ the Kinsmen Redeemer. Christ has taken us from a lost and hopeless place to a place of exaltation. We are seated with Christ in heavenly places. He has given us every promise of God, which are yes and amen. There are many prophetic pictures being revealed to us in the New Covenant. The whole purpose of God in choosing a bride for His Son was just as Eve had intimacy with her husband without shame so also the bride of Christ can walk in a deep union and communion with Christ without shame.

The Ketubah, the marriage covenant and the Mohar, the bridal price is used in the example of Abraham. "When Abraham's servant heard what they said, he bowed down to the ground before the Lord. Then the servant brought out gold and silver jewelry and articles of clothing and gave them to Rebekah; he also gave costly gifts to her brother and to her mother" (Genesis 24:52–53). The Ketubah and the Mohar are inseparable.

Abraham knew that a bridal price and a contract would be needed when looking for a wife for his son. Abraham brought out all kinds of extravagant articles, gold, silver, and garments, because he was negotiating a price for an acceptable bride for his son. Therefore, Abraham was extravagant in his payment. We will see how extravagant the payment was that the Lord Jesus made for us.

As a negotiated price, the promise of the bridegroom was that he would love his bride unconditionally and he would love her extravagantly. He promised that he would provide for her, protect her, care for her, and cherish her. As these promises are brought before Rebekah, she would also have responsibility in this contract. This marital contract was a covenant. A covenant is a sacred agreement between two parties, which is guaranteed and the contract cannot be broken. That was God's intention for man. That is why Jesus said, "What God has joined together let no man separate."

As Rebekah saw these promises she had to come into agreement with these promises and she had a responsibility herself. Her responsibilities were that she would love her husband; she would surrender herself completely to him, as well as a complete yieldedness to his leadership and authority. She was willing to say, "I am yours, every part of me, all that I am and all that I have is yours." That was the contract.

The bridal price as negotiated was extravagant. He brought out gold, silver and articles of clothing. He brought out the best he had because he wanted an acceptable bride for his son. It wasn't cheap.

We are going to look at a passage of Scripture that is often used in relation to husbands loving their wives. It is a passage that speaks about the husband's responsibility to love the wife. But this passage is so much more than that. It is a passage that prophetically describes the mystery that is being revealed that pertains to Christ and His church. "Husbands, love your wives, just as Christ loved the church and gave himself up for her to make her holy, cleansing her by the washing with water through the word, and to present her to himself as a radiant church, without stain or wrinkle or any other blemish, but holy and blameless. In this same way, husbands ought to love their wives as their own bodies. He who loves his wife loves himself. After all, no one ever hated their own body, but they feed and care for their body, just as Christ does the church— for we are members of his body. "For this reason a man will leave his father and mother and be united to his wife, and the two will become one flesh." This is a profound mystery—but I am talking about Christ and the church. However, each one of you also must love his wife as he loves himself, and the wife must respect her husband" (Ephesians 5:25–33). Some versions may say this is a great mystery that is now being revealed to you, that first and foremost, Christ loves His bride.

Husbands, love your wives as Christ loved the church. Jesus absolutely loves you. He loves you extravagantly, he loves you passionately, He loves you unconditionally. Christ never said to you, "Hey, wait a minute, clean your act up before you could come." He didn't say, "Man you really messed up, I'm not accepting you until you get clean." No! He accepted you and loved you right where you were at. He accepted me when I was at the lowest of the low and it was pretty low. He loved you sacrificially. The bridal payment is extravagant. "For you know that it was not with perishable things such as silver or gold that you were redeemed from the empty way of life handed down to you from your ancestors, but with the precious blood of Christ, a lamb without blemish or defect" (1 Peter 1:18). You were brought with a price and that price is the precious, priceless, blood of Jesus Christ. Far more priceless than any gold or silver, which He owns it all anyway. He loves you with a sacrificial love. He was willing to give up His life, He was willing to be beaten beyond human recognition. And be stripped naked, bare, for all to see. The humiliation! He was willing to be spat on, His beard plucked out, beaten with rods and fists, because of His great love for you, because of His great love for me. He loves you eternally. Scripture says, "I have loved you with an everlasting love." He loves you passionately. Can you say this, "Jesus loves me. Jesus loves me extravagantly. Jesus loves me passionately. Jesus' love for me is a consuming love. His love for me is an intimate love. Jesus' love for me is a precious, passionate love. He loves me. HE LOVES ME." Say it louder, "HE LOVES ME! HE LOVES ME! HE LOVES ME! HE LOVES ME!"

Did you get it? I can't tell you how many people say, "I just don't feel like God loves me anymore." Do you realize God does not love you because of what you do or don't do? He doesn't love you any more than He does now, because He already loves you in all of His fullness. Did you know He cannot love you any less because the fullness of His nature is love? No matter what you do or don't do, He cannot love you any less because that would determine that He is not who He is. He is love. He loves you only because He chose to love you, not because of anything that you are, not because you are wise or beautiful, not because your handsome, or smart, not because you are good. He loves you because that is His nature to love you, passionately, extravagantly, in all of His fullness. He loves you just because He chose to love you and it never diminishes—never! The problem isn't with Him; it's that your heart is not opened wide. The relationship takes two. You can have a spouse love you passionately and extravagantly and if you are cold and detached not wanting to receive their love, not wanting to be loved, you won't feel loved. But on God's side, His love for you is magnificent, extravagant, zealous, and unending.

Notice that it says, "Just as Christ also loved the church and gave Himself up for her, so that He might sanctify her, having cleansed her by the washing of water with the word." The word *sanctify* means "to be set apart." There are three aspects to sanctification. The first aspect is positional. The moment you trusted Christ, He set you apart from sin and He set you apart to Himself. In other words, he paid the bridal price. The bridal price was His precious body was broken and His blood shed. He gave Himself up for you to sanctify you, to set you apart from sin, to set you apart for Himself. In the same way, a bride would be set apart for her husband waiting for the time when they would be consummated in their love for one another, in the marriage ceremony and in the marriage bed. The word sanctify also carries the idea of a progressive sanctification. It means that as the Holy Spirit begins to work in you and begins to set you apart continually from your sin patterns and habits. He is continuously setting you apart from sin and setting you apart to Himself. This happens by the washing of water of the word of God. You will never grow spiritually if you are not in the Word. It is the Word of God that sanctifies, cleanses, and washes our minds. I can promise you, some of us need a brain washing. It is the word of God that washes, shapes, and renews. It is the word of God that shapes our character; it is the word of God that formulates our values. It is the word of God that teaches us how to say no to ungodliness and yes to righteousness. It is the word of God, by the Spirit of God that brings to life, giving us fresh revelation every day.

Finally, the third aspect of sanctification is Ultimate sanctification. It is the love of God that wants you set apart for Him. The moment your faith is made sight either through death or through the rapture, you are forever set apart to Him, never to taste the sting of death, or sin again. It is His love that accomplished this at Calvary. It is in His love that He would present the church in all her glory having no spot or wrinkle or any such thing. She, the church, would be holy and blameless.

"So husbands ought also to love their own wives as their own bodies. He who loves his own wife loves himself." Just as a husband should care for his wife, so also Christ cares for His bride. He cares for His bride because He is our provider. It says in Philippians 4:19 that "He will supply all our needs according to His riches in glory." In Matthew 6:25–34, Jesus also tells us we should not worry about what we should eat or drink because our Heavenly Father knows that we have needs of such things but seek first the kingdom of God and His righteousness and all these things will be added to you. He protects His bride. "You are kept by the power of God, ready to be revealed in that last day" (1 Peter 1:5). You are protected by His grace! Nothing shall separate you from the love of God, neither death, nor life, nor angels or demons, nor things above or things below. No created thing is able to keep you or separate you from the love of Christ, which is in Christ Jesus our Lord (Romans 8:38–39). Nothing can separate you. You are in His grip. He paid the bridal price, you belong to Jesus. "Or do you not know that your body is a temple of the Holy Spirit who is in you, whom you have from God, and that you are not your own? For you have been bought with a price: therefore glorify God in your body" (1 Cor. 6:20). You belong to Him. Paid for by His own blood, taking you out of the kingdom of darkness and taking you out of the shame, condemnation, brokenness, out of eternal death, and judgment, into the glorious light of the kingdom of God. Forever! Wow, that is amazing! He loves you with a love that nourishes and cherishes. Just as He feeds us with the manna of the Word of God, He also nourishes us through the Spirit of God, through His sweet presence. Our soul and spirit are nourished as we drink from the fountain, the water of life. He nourishes us through His presence, His Spirit. The living water that Jesus was talking about at the well with the woman, "If you drink this water you will never thirst again" (John 4:14) is the refreshment that the Holy Spirit gives. He cherishes you! He is the lover of your soul! He is your bridegroom! His love is so extravagant!

Finally it says, "For this reason a man shall leave his father and mother and be joined to his wife and the two shall become one flesh, this mystery is great but I am speaking in reference to Christ and His church." The word *joined* carries the idea of a bond that cannot be broken. The covenant that Christ has established for us is like taking two pieces of wood, gluing them together and pressing them together. It cannot be separated. If you tried, the wood would splinter apart. The whole idea is that you are in an unbreakable, love covenant with God. His love for you is an unbreakable bond that cannot be broken. He will never leave you, He will never forsake you, you are always in His grip, you are His favorite one. Can you say that? "I am His favorite one!" Oh, and by the way, I am too, because He loves His church, His bride. We are His favorite ones!

There is a responsibility we have in the covenantal contract. His contract to you says, "I will love you even if you turn your back on me. I'll still love you!" You may not be able to experience that love because your back is turned, but He still loves you. He still loves you even when you say you don't want to love Him. You are still in His grip, even though you may be walking the other way.

Do you know how many Christians are missing out on the extravagant joy of the Master's love? What is our responsibility? This passage is really part of the same; it's a prophetic picture of the bride of Christ and Christ the bridegroom. "Wives be subject to your own husband as onto the Lord for the husband is the head of the wife just as Christ is the head of the church; He himself being Savior of the body but as the church is subject to Christ, wives ought to be subject to the husband in everything." Here we see a prophetic picture of the relationship between the wife and her husband and the bride (the church) to her husband who is Christ. What is our responsibility? Jesus says he who loves Me obeys my commandments (John 14:15). What are the commandments? The greatest commandment is, "'YOU SHALL LOVE THE LORD YOUR GOD WITH ALL YOUR HEART, AND WITH ALL YOUR SOUL, AND WITH ALL YOUR MIND.' This is the great and foremost commandment. The second is like it, 'YOU SHALL

LOVE YOUR NEIGHBOR AS YOURSELF'" (Mt. 22:38–39). Just as Jesus is pouring out all the time all His extravagant love to us, we can be receivers of His love as we love Him back. It's not just a Sunday thing, or not just a Monday thing, or Tuesday thing. It is not going to church on Sunday and then doing what you want to do the rest of the week. It is "Jesus I give you all!" It is complete submission, being completely yielded. It is, "God, I let you have Your own way in my life. All that I am, all that I have, all that I ever hope to be is in You." That is our only appropriate response. When you totally surrender, something amazing takes place. The warmth and the fellowship of His presence begins to envelope you. As you give Him praise, as you begin to love on Him, as You begin to tell Him how magnificent He is, how glorious and radiant He is, He manifests His love in a tangible way. "Draw near to God and He will draw near to you" (Jas. 4:8). It's His love He wants for each of us. It's the enemy that wants you to close your heart against the love of God.

Some of you have been afflicted with deep hurts from the past, some of you like me had fathers that abandoned you, or maybe they were just absent, some abusive. The enemy wants you to look at your father who is broken, weak and imperfect and make you think that that is what your heavenly Father is like. This is simply not true. It is a lie from the pit of hell. His banner over you is love. Your bridegroom Jesus wants to walk with you just as Eve walked with her husband in the cool of the garden, without shame, complete intimate, union, and communion with Him. All you have to do is so simple and so profound, open up your heart and receive, "Here I am, Lord, I give you my all, all that I have, all that I want, all that I ever hope to be."

What do you need to give to your Savior? What do you need to give to your Bridegroom? His love is extravagant for you. He has withheld nothing from you. He has blessed you beyond measure and He is calling out to you for a deep, abiding, love relationship. I can tell you that for most Christian's, their prayer life is, "Lord, I have a problem" or "Lord, I want this" or "Lord, help." Prayer is not to be a one-way street. "My sheep hear my voice and they follow Me" (Jn.

10:27). Our prayer time should be loving on Him, having Him love on you, telling Him how magnificent He is. Him telling you how magnificent you are, and you are magnificent. You are brilliant! You are beautiful! You are lovely! You are incredible! You are the crowning glory of God's creation. All of you who are in Christ are clothed with white garments, justified (declared righteous) by the blood of Jesus. All of you have a measure of Christ's authority. You are seated with Christ in heavenly places (Eph. 2:6). You are a king, a priest, a child of royalty, children of the most high God, who is the King of kings and Lord of lords. You are amazing and some of you may not even realize it yet.

What do you need to turn over? What do you need to do? What do you need to give up? I can promise you this, the deposit you get from Him is exceedingly, abundantly, above all we could ever ask or imagine when we surrender. If you have never yet trusted the Lord Jesus, I can promise you that He is a bridegroom that is extravagant in His love for you. You may be one of those that He is drawing near. You may be one of those that you feel that pull in your heart and yet you have not come yet. Scripture is so clear that God demonstrates His love for us in that while we were sinners Christ died for us. He died for you, He satisfied the bridal price, and He is drawing you to Himself. I can promise you as a person who was rescued from the dung heap of sin and brokenness, that there is no greater delight than to be loved by Him. There is no human relationship that can be as close or as intimate. There is no human relationship that can satisfy as Jesus can satisfy. He has called you to be set free from the kingdom of darkness, forgiven of every sin and into an eternal covenant relationship with the Father forever. Jesus as your bridegroom wants you to be in union and communion forever. Again, remember it's not sexual but it is a deep, abiding, covenant, in union and communion with him. If you have not trusted Christ, I invite you to do so today. Just pray this simple prayer, "Lord, I confess that I am a sinner." Just tell him, "Lord, I know I've sinned against you. I know I've been rebellious. I confess the cursing that has come out of my mouth. I confess the bitterness that has been in my heart. I confess the pride and the rebellion that is there. I leave it at the Cross. I accept Jesus as my personal Savior and Lord. I believe and accept that Jesus died for me, I believe and accept that He rose triumphantly from the grave. Forgive my sins. I thank you and I accept the gift of eternal life."

CHAPTER 5

The Mikveh: Ritual Immersion

We have been working through the prophetic picture of the ancient wedding ceremony of Israel. What we have discovered is that this ancient Jewish wedding ceremony gives us an incredible, powerful, prophetic picture of Christ the bridegroom and His bride the Church.

Now we are going to study the Mikveh, which literally means "the immersion." Even though we do not see in Scripture the Mikveh ceremony, it was an important part of the wedding ceremony and it is still today.

There are many reasons for the Mikveh; for instance, when a priest was to be consecrated, they were immersed in water. The Mikveh was an identification that they were being set apart from their former way of life and being set apart for service to God. It also meant that they were now ritually cleansed; they were now holy. A person who had leprosy, if they were healed, they would be required to participate in the Mikveh. They would be immersed in water and that symbolized that they were "set apart" from their uncleanness, that they were set apart for God and that they were holy. After Jesus healed the person with leprosy, He said go and wash in the pool and then show yourself to the priest. Then the priest, when he learned he was healed and participated in the Mikveh, he would say, "You are clean." This meant he could be integrated back into society. If you touched a dead person in ancient Israel, you would be considered unclean. The unclean person would have to participate in the Mikveh. He was ritually immersed, which meant he is now set apart from his uncleanness and set apart to God and that he was holy. A woman after her menstrual cycle, did the same thing, she would participate in the Mikveh. This too meant she was set apart from her uncleanness and set apart for her husband.

The Mikveh was also used very importantly in the wedding ceremony for both the bride and the groom, but they did not participate at the same time. The groom, when he participated in the Mikveh, was demonstrating that he was being set apart from his former matter of life, from being single to being set apart for his bride; he would be her one and only. It also demonstrated that he was pure, that he was holy. The bride, on the other hand, she, too, participated in the Mikveh. She was immersed and set apart from her former life of being single, set apart to her husband, and she was his one and only. She too was now holy. She was now set apart for her new life as his wife. She would be given a new identity as she became one with her husband and assumed his name.

In the New Testament, we find that the Mikveh is nothing more than baptism. "For I do not want you to be unaware, brethren, that our fathers were all under the cloud and all passed through the sea; and all were baptized into Moses in the cloud and in the sea" (1 Cor. 10:1–2). Here, Paul calls the Mikveh of the Old Covenant, baptism. It is the same thing, the word *baptize* means "to immerse," specifically to immerse in water.

When Israel was leaving the land of slavery and going to the promise land, they were being chased by the Egyptians. They were being protected with a cloud by day and a pillar of fire by night. To be baptized in the cloud was merely to be immersed in God's presence, but it was in the sea that they were immersed. Their immersion was an identification. They were identified with Moses as having him as their leader and spiritual father. It was also a setting apart from their former matter of life of slavery and being set apart to a new way of life of freedom. It was also a ritual cleansing because these folks had placed their hope in the Passover lamb. The lamb that was slain and the blood that was spilled was placed on the door post and the lintel. As they trusted in the blood of the lamb it symbolized Messiah who would come and spill His blood as the atoning sacrifice for their sins. As they were immersed in water, it demonstrated that they were now cleansed, holy and moving forward into a land of freedom and prosperity.

It is important to understand that baptism in the Old Covenant was very, very important. Baptism in the New Covenant is also very, very important because it is an outward symbol of an inward reality. "Then Jesus arrived from Galilee at the Jordan coming to John, to be baptized by him. But John tried to prevent Him, saying, "I have need to be baptized by You, and do You come to me?" But Jesus answering said to him, "Permit it at this time; for in this way it is fitting for us to fulfill all righteousness." Then he permitted Him" (Matt. 3:13–15). This is the first instance in the New Testament that we see Baptism according to the Old Covenant. This is a baptism of repentance. As discussed earlier, there were many reasons for the Mikveh in the Old Covenant. It simply means "to be immersed." John the Baptist is giving them a baptism of repentance or Mikveh of repentance. John is calling the people of Israel to be set apart from their sin and to set themselves apart for Messiah who is to come. John the Baptist is to prepare the way of Messiah. He is not only calling them out of rebellion and sin but preparing them for the righteousness that Messiah would provide. That is why John was confused. John sees Jesus coming and the Spirit of God reveals to him that this is the Lamb of God that came to take away the sins of the world. This is the sinless, spotless Lamb of God, this is the Holy One. John says, "I need to be baptized by you." He didn't understand that there was another reason for the Mikveh. In fact, he says in another place: "I am not even worthy to untie your shoes." John was thinking, you are a holy man that does not need to repent.

Notice Jesus said, "It is fitting for us to fulfill all righteousness." Jesus is declaring that He is being set apart for His bride. Jesus was being set apart to fulfill all righteousness.

Jesus was making a public declaration that He is the righteous one, that He is the Messiah, that He is the One who will provide righteousness to those that trust in Him. It's the Mikveh. Just as the bridegroom would prepare for his bride, Jesus in essence, was preparing Himself for the church, which is His bride. He is saying, I am being set apart to my bride. I am the bridegroom, holy, blameless, set apart, and prepared to lead My bride.

Even today, we celebrate the Mikveh and it is extremely important. "And Jesus came up and spoke to them, saying, 'All authority has been given to Me in heaven and on earth. Go therefore and make disciples of all the nations, baptizing them in the name of the Father and the Son and the Holy Spirit, teaching them to observe all that I commanded you; and lo, I am with you always, even to the end of the age'" (Mt. 28:18–20). Notice, the first phrase, Jesus said, "All authority in heaven and earth has been given to me." Do you know what that means? It means He's the boss. There is no one greater. He is the boss of everyone in heaven. He is the boss of everyone here on earth and over all the angels. He is the boss over demons, even the ones who are already in the abyss. He is the boss of everyone saved and unsaved. He has all authority in heaven and on earth and under the earth. There is no one greater, there is no one who has supreme authority over Him, He has all authority.

Do you know what that means for the unbeliever, the ones who reject Christ? That means that every one of them is going to stand before the great, white, throne of judgment and they will meet Him as judge. He will say to them, "Depart from me you worker of iniquity and enter into eternal torment." God will cast them into the lake of fire (Rev. 20:14–15). Do you know what that means for every demon? Do you know what that means for Satan himself? It means that they also will stand in front of the throne of judgment and they will be cast into the Lake of Fire forever.

Do you know what that means for you and I as believers in Christ? It means that we are in relationship with Him forever. Our punishment has been met by Christ on the cross. He called us into a deep loving relationship with Christ. Do you realize how privileged we are? God says to us, because He is in authority over us, "Go, make disciples of all nations." A disciple is a learner and a follower of Christ. We are not just called to win the lost, although that is part of it. Our bridegroom, the one who loves us with an everlasting love, the one who has called us into this intimate love relationship with Him is saying, "Go, make disciples." Win the lost, build them up in the faith, equip them to do the work of the ministry. He is calling us to spiritually multiply, to bear fruit. Then God says, "Baptize them in the name of the Father, Son, and Holy Spirit, teaching them to observe all that I have commanded you and lo, I am with you always even to the end of the age." Baptize them, immerse them, the Mikveh. Notice that once they are baptized then we are commanded to teach them all that He had taught them to do.

Here in America, we hate the word *command*. This country was founded on rebellion. The American spirit is really a spirit of rebellion. It's a spirit of wanting to do what we want to do when we want to do it. It's wanting to be like God. It's wanting to have control over your own destiny and no one can tell you what to do. "I'm free, after all," we say. We are free; the problem is that we do not understand what freedom is. Freedom doesn't mean that we have the right to do whatever we want to do. For instance, if everyone had the right to do whatever everyone wanted to do we would call that anarchy. Freedom always has constraints; it always has boundaries. For instance, if I don't like my friend today and I choose in my own freedom to whack him, then I infringed on His freedoms. If I whack him with a 9mm, what do you think is going to happen to me? The police will arrest me. I can't say, "Wait a minute, I'm free!" Well, I won't be anymore. I would be locked up. Why? Because freedom does not mean we get to do what we want to do. Freedom means that we have the ability to choose to please God. If we choose to rebel against God we find ourselves in bondage as slaves to sin.

Many believers look at that passage of Scripture and think that this is optional. If I feel like it I will make disciples. But if we Love God with all our heart, soul, mind and strength and love our brother as ourselves, then we will want to make disciples. We will see that the heartbeat of God is to seek after the lost. To love God and others is to fulfill all the commandments of God. The whole Bible can be reduced into those two commands. This is because Jesus has called us to a love relationship with Him. Then to love Him, if we are truly a disciple, a lover, a learner and follower of Christ, if we are truly born again and made alive, we will want to be in a fellowship relationship with Him. We want to love Him, we will want to give Him all that we are. If we truly love Him, then we will do what He says. Jesus said, "Why call me Lord, Lord if you are unwilling to do what I say?" (Luke 6:46) If we truly love Him we are going to be completely surrendered to Him. If we truly love God, we will want to walk with Him, we will want to talk with Him, we will want to enjoy Him. If we truly love Him we will want to give Him the glory He deserves.

It's not about obeying a list of dos and don'ts. It's about being enamored with Him, being affectionate to Him; He is our bride-groom after all. If we truly love God, we will truly love one another. If we truly love God then we will love the lost. Then spiritual multiplication doesn't become a problem because we know their need is Jesus. Fear will no longer be a factor because perfect love casts out all fear. Now, I am no longer worried about what others think of me or the rejection I face or the persecution I might receive. It's all about loving that person who is lost and needs Jesus. If we truly love people then we will honor them and speak kindly to them or speak kindly about them. If we truly love people, we will put them before our own selfish desires, think kind thoughts of them, because love bares all things, believes all things, hopes all things, and endures all things.

Most really don't understand what the great commandment is. It is not so much about don't doing, it's about do. Do love God, do love each other, do speak kindly, do treat one another with honor, do love the lost. We see this so clearly in the Mikveh and why it is so important. "What shall we say then? Are we to continue in sin so that grace may increase? May it never be! How shall we who died to sin still live in it? Or do you not know that all of us who have been baptized into Christ Jesus have been baptized into His death? Therefore we have been buried with Him through baptism into death, so that as Christ was raised from the dead through the glory of the Father, so we too might walk in newness of life. For if we have become united with Him in the likeness of His death, certainly we shall also be in the likeness of His resurrection (Romans 6:1–5). What Paul is describing is that when we are baptized we are declaring who we are in Christ. The moment you trusted Christ you died to self. The moment you trusted Christ your old nature was put to death. You have been made alive to Jesus Christ and have received His divine nature. Baptism is a declaration that I am separated from the world system and separated from the kingdom of darkness, separated from my old way of life. I am separated from the life of rebellion and pride and I have been made alive. I've been born again. I am separated to Christ, I belong to Him, He paid the price. I've been brought with a price, the price of the blood of the New Covenant, the price that Jesus paid with His own death, burial and resurrection. I am identifying with Him, I am identifying with the fact that He died for me and therefore I also died. Myself is dead. The old man of who I was is dead. The old nature is gone and obliterated, buried with Christ. Now I have been made alive, I have been given His divine nature. "For by these He has granted to us His precious and magnificent promises, so that by them you may become partakers of the divine nature, having escaped the corruption that is in the world by lust" (2 Peter 1:4).

This identification, this Mikveh, this baptism is really a public declaration that you are a new man in Christ. It is a declaration that you have been brought into a covenant relationship with the bridegroom Jesus. You belong to Him, you no longer belong to the world system, you are no longer a child of the devil, you are no longer a child of wrath. You're the King's kid, you're the bride. This causes Paul to ask two important questions, the first question, what shall we say then? Are we to continue in sin so that grace may increase? Apparently, during Paul's day there were a group of people that believed, like many today, that somehow you can glorify God by living as you please. Chapter 6 of Romans comes after chapters 4 and 5. Chapter 4 speaks about the righteousness we gain though faith and chapter 5 speaks about how we are declared righteous and justified by grace through faith in the Lord Jesus Christ. If I am justified I am declared righteous, I am innocent, sinless in the Father's eyes. I am sanctified, justified, and glorified all in one, meaning I am in His grip and nothing can separate me from the love of God. The false theology or philosophy is that now I can live as I please. Paul says in the strongest language, No, may it never be! Why? Do you not know that all of us who have been baptized into Christ Jesus have been baptized into His death. Therefore, we have been buried with Him through baptism into death, so that as Christ was raised from the dead through the glory of the Father, so we too might walk in newness of life.

Now Paul will give you three arguments against to why this philosophy is indeed false. The first reason is your new identity. It is not who you are, you are not a sinner, you're a saint. Do you know that even to the Corinthians who were dealing with all sorts of sin in the church, and yet he called them saints, he called them beloved? We are no longer sinners, we are no longer part of this world; we are aliens and strangers. We are no longer a people without hope, we are no longer a people without God in the world and we are no longer separated from Him. We are no longer apart from the promises of God. We are co-heirs with Christ. We are now people of God who have all the promises of God, which are yes and amen. We have it all. The first reason is that we don't live like the world lives is because we are not of the world. We are not people who have to live in darkness; we are people who have been called out of darkness and into light.

Once again, it is not about rules and regulations; it's not about dos and don'ts. It's about whether you're going to love God and others and put self to death. It's not about you. You died; stop trying to resurrect an old corpse. Every relational problem comes from selfishness. It is because we don't understand who we are. The only right we have in this world is to love God and love each other. Your rights were purchased at the cross.

The second thing that is important to know is that sin has been defeated. "Knowing this, that our old self was crucified with Him, in order that our body of sin might be done away with, so that we would no longer be slaves to sin; for he who has died is freed from sin (Romans 6:6–7). As we trusted Christ something amazing happened. Not only did the old man die but sin was put to death. Some of you may be saying, "But I still struggle." You're right, the reason why you still struggle is because you have these habits that have been in place, some of you for years and years and years. The bottom line is this: you and I have a choice that the unbeliever does not have.

When Adam and Eve were first created, they were created sinless. Because they were created sinless, they had a free will. This is important to understand. That meant that they had the choice to please God, to worship Him, to walk with Him in the garden, to enjoy communion with Him. They had the privilege of joining in the most intimate union with God. They walked with Him; they did it. They only had one thing that they could not do. They could have chosen the tree of life and lived forever but they chose the tree of the knowledge of good and evil and the moment that happened something died inside them. At that moment, everything changed. They took fig leaves to cover their shame and nakedness. This is the first institution of religion, which is man's futile attempt to deal with his sin problem. Then they ran and hid from God because that is what shame and guilt does, it always causes you to run. The moment that happened, every person after Adam and Eve was born spiritually dead. They were not born with a free will like Adam and Eve. You have to get that false theology out of your head. They were born with a corrupted will, a will that shakes it's fist at God, a will that says, "I want to do what I want to do." In Ephesians 2:1–3 it says, "As for you, you were dead in your trespasses in which you used to live when you followed the ways of the world and of the ruler of the king of the air, the spirit who is now at work in the sons of disobedience. All of us at that time, gratifying our sinful nature and following our desires and thoughts. We were by nature objects of wrath." That's who we were, children of wrath. We were part of the kingdom of darkness. In John 8:44, Jesus said to the Pharisees, "You are of your father the devil." That's what we were, children of the devil doing what the devil wanted us to do. Living according to our lusts and desires, doing what we wanted to do. We have not had a free will until Christ. The moment you trusted Christ, you became the new Adam, the Adam that was justified, sanctified, and set apart and glorified. Now we have a choice. We now have the ability to love God, to choose to please Him, to choose to submit to Him, to choose to enjoy Him, or we could choose rebellion. Now we have a choice.

Paul is saying, "Don't live as though you are dead. Don't live your life as if you are in slavery because you have been set free." The idea behind why baptism is important is because you are declaring you left your former matter of life, that you have been set free from the slavery of sin, that you have been set free from the kingdom of darkness. Your identity is that you are a new man, a child of God, you are holy, pure, lovely, brilliant; the bride of Christ and you will live for Him. That's what it's all about. When you live for Him, you're going to love Him, give Him your all, worship Him, you are going to submit to Him and everything else falls right into place. As you love Him, you receive the love of God and as you receive the love of God you cannot help but to love each other. If you cannot love someone who you can see, you cannot love Him whom you cannot see.

Every relationship in your human life is predicated on your relationship with Jesus. That's what it's all about, it's about Him. It's about choosing. Paul says, "Do you not know that when you present yourselves to someone as slaves for obedience, you are slaves of the one whom you obey, either of sin resulting in death, or of obedience resulting in righteousness?" (Romans 6:16) The only act of obedience we have is loving God and loving others. That is all that really matters, everything else will fall into place.

If you are believer and have not been baptized by immersion for any reason, you're in rebellion. It's a commandment. What child of God that has been delivered from the kingdom of darkness does not want to identify with his King, with his bridegroom? People around the world are dying because they are unafraid to publicly declare that they have been set apart from sin and set apart for Jesus Christ. It is costly to Jewish people, their families declare them dead, and they cut them from their lives just because they publicly declared their submission to the leadership of Christ and identified with Him. In Muslim countries, they could be executed. Here in America, it doesn't cost us anything. As a child of God, we have to start thinking with a kingdom mind-set. We have to get rid of that independent American spirit that say, "I have the right to do whatever I want to do." We don't, we only have one right, to love God and love people. If we do that I can promise you we will walk in favor of God. Fear is your greatest enemy. Fear is one aspect the enemy uses to destroy relationships. You have to put fear to death. It's not who you are; it's a dead corpse. You can't enjoy God's love if you don't love Him back and you can't enjoy Him if you are at odds with your brother or sister. Bitterness will absolutely wreck your life. Fear will wreck your life. You have no right to have it anyway.

CHAPTER 6

The Eyrusin: Betrothal

The Eyrusin is the betrothal period. The betrothal period was an important part of the wedding ceremony. It always began with giving vows to one another. It was the establishment of the covenant the bride and groom were making together. Once the vows were said, the bride and groom would share a cup of wine which sealed the deal. The moment they drank that cup, they were considered legally married; the only way out of it was either through death or divorce. This is why when Joseph learned Mary was pregnant, he was going to divorce her quietly. He was going to divorce her quietly because he didn't want her to be shamed, humiliated, or worse, possibly put to death by stoning.

When the angel showed up and revealed to Joseph that what happened to Mary was by the Holy Spirit, Joseph then took Mary to be his wife. He consummated the marriage after the baby was born. The marriage contract was legally binding. They were considered married, but the bride and groom were not permitted to live together.

The betrothal period was considered to be an indefinite period although it generally lasted between nine and twelve months. In this process, there were three things that would take place. The bridegroom would tell the bride that "I am going away for a time, but I will be back for you." While he was away, he would build a home for the both of them. This was usually built on his father's property, and it had to be the very best home he could afford and it had to be approved by his father. If the father did not approve of the home he built, then he could not collect his bride, because it would be the father that would be shamed if it was not up to par. The second thing that takes place is that the bridegroom leaves a helper for the bride, which was usually a friend and he would make sure the bride was provided for and protected. When the time had come, the helper would go with the bridegroom to collect his bride. The third thing that took place is that the bride had to make herself ready for the bridegroom. The betrothal period was a time for her to learn how to love her husband. During this time, she would learn the necessary skills of being a good wife. She knew the bridegroom was coming back for her, but she didn't know when this was going to take place. She knew the approximate time but she did not know the day or the hour of the bridegroom's return. Therefore, she was always prepared. The closer the time came for his return, she would be waiting expectantly. She would be waiting joyfully, she would be waiting for her bridegroom to take her and bring her into his home to consummate that marriage.

There is an amazing parallel between the betrothal ceremony and Christ the bridegroom and His bride the church. In the betrothal ceremony, the groom and the bride would share a cup of wine. That would seal the marital contract and make it legally binding. What is fascinating is this is what was taking place at the last supper, in preparation of Jesus paying the Mohar, the bridal price. At the last supper, Jesus taking the cup said, "But I say to you, I will not drink of this fruit of the vine from now on until that day when I drink it new with you in My Father's kingdom" (Matt. 26:29). It was at this last supper that Jesus said, "This is my body which will be broken for you, do this in remembrance of me." It was the bread that demonstrated a symbol that Christ's death was the bridal payment for us, His bride. It was His death on the cross that would pay the penalty for our sins so that our sins may be forgiven. When Jesus said, "This is the cup of the New Covenant of My blood, do this in remembrance of Me." It was this promise that Jesus was making that by His stripes we are healed, by His shed blood we would be washed, cleansed, justified, and forgiven as we exercise faith in Him. It was this covenant that Jesus was making with the church. Then He shared the cup with the brethren.

Notice what Jesus says, "I will not drink of the fruit of this vine from now on." Why? Why would He not drink of the fruit of the vine until He comes into His Father's kingdom? We know that after the day of His resurrection until the day of His ascension, those forty days that he walked on the earth that Jesus was with His brethren. Jesus is not going to share that cup until the Marriage Supper of the Lamb when this union is consummated with His bride, just as it is in the same way in the marital covenant between a bride and her groom. Jesus establishes His covenant, then He seals the deal by the sharing of His cup. Jesus establishes a promise. The promise is that although He goes away He will return. "And as they were gazing intently into the sky while He was going, behold, two men in white clothing stood beside them. They also said, 'Men of Galilee, why do you stand looking into the sky? This Jesus, who has been taken up from you into heaven, will come in just the same way as you have watched Him go into heaven'" (Acts 1:10–11). This takes place forty days after the resurrection. We call this the Day of Ascension. This is the day that Jesus is taken up to heaven, this is the day that the disciples saw Him leave and they were frightened. They were confused and they wondered, "Has He left us orphaned? Is this the end of us, are we on our own? What's to become of us?"

Jesus had promised He was going to go away but He was going to come back and receive them to Himself. They stood there watching as Jesus was taken into heaven and an angel appeared and said, "Hey, He is coming back for you." The bridegroom is coming back for His bride. What is the bridegroom doing? Notice what Jesus Himself said in John 14:1–3, "Do not let your heart be troubled; believe in God, believe also in Me. In My Father's house are many dwelling places;

if it were not so, I would have told you; for I go to prepare a place for you. If I go and prepare a place for you, I will come again and receive you to Myself, that where I am, there you may be also." What is Jesus the Bridegroom doing? He is preparing a home for His bride. Some of your Bible versions may say *mansions*. For example, the King James Version uses the word *mansions* but the word means "dwelling place." Try to understand why the King James version writers used the word mansions. Do you know why? Because what Jesus is preparing makes everything on earth look like a garbage can.

Our bridegroom is preparing a home for us. As you read the following passage try to imagine this home that Jesus is preparing. As you read this, you will come across some precious stones. These stones are the most priceless, purist, of different colors, the purist of the pure, that reflect the light of Jesus Christ like a prism. "'Come here, I will show you the bride, the wife of the Lamb.' And he carried me away in the Spirit to a great and high mountain, and showed me the holy city, Jerusalem, coming down out of heaven from God, having the glory of God. Her brilliance was like a very costly stone, as a stone of crystal-clear jasper. It had a great and high wall, with twelve gates, and at the gates twelve angels; and names were written on them, which are the names of the twelve tribes of the sons of Israel. There were three gates on the east and three gates on the north and three gates on the south and three gates on the west. [14]And the wall of the city had twelve foundation stones, and on them were the twelve names of the twelve apostles of the Lamb. The one who spoke with me had a gold measuring rod to measure the city, and its gates and its wall. The city is laid out as a square, and its length is as great as the width; and he measured the city with the rod, fifteen hundred miles; its length and width and height are equal. And he measured its wall, seventy-two yards, according to human measurement which are also angelic measurements. The material of the wall was jasper; and the city was pure gold, like clear glass. The foundation stones of the city wall were adorned with every kind of precious stone. The first foundation stone was jasper; the second, sapphire; the third, chalcedony; the fourth, emerald; the fifth, sardonyx; the sixth, sardis; the seventh, chrysolite; the eighth, beryl; the ninth, topaz; the tenth, chrysoprase; the eleventh, jacinth; the twelfth, amethyst. And the twelve gates were twelve pearls; each one of the gates was a single pearl. And the street of the city was pure gold, like transparent glass. I saw no temple in it, for the Lord God the Almighty and the Lamb are its temple. And the city has no need of the sun or of the moon to shine on it, for the glory of God has illumined it, and its lamp is the Lamb. The nations will walk by its light, and the kings of the earth will bring their glory into it. In the daytime (for there will be no night there) its gates will never be closed; and they will bring the glory and the honor of the nations into it; and nothing unclean, and no one who practices abomination and lying, shall ever come into it, but only those whose names are written in the Lamb's book of life" (Rev. 21:9–27).

Remember, it is the bridegroom's responsibility to prepare a home for his bride with the best he could possibly afford. If he didn't give the absolute best the father would be shamed. The home that Jesus, our bridegroom is preparing for us is a home that is so magnificent, that the glory of God will just radiate. Picture the prism of different colors off every precious stone, over every building made of solid gold, over the streets that are so pure that it is translucent. The glory of God is manifested in ways we cannot even fathom.

In Revelation 22, it speaks about the tree of life that is in the middle of the city. Let me suggest to you that even though the passage does not describe for us all that is there, let me share with you that probably, every exotic plant, tree, and flower of every color, and every kind is there. This place is the most beautiful, magnificent and glorious place that your mind can't even imagine. There will be colors that we have never even seen before that will be manifested in this place. This isn't even the best part. The best part is this, that you will be able to see God in all of His glory and majesty face-to-face. The magnificence of the place where we are going to is so absolutely incredible and that is not even the best. The best is Him. All of the light that is reflecting off the gold and the precious jewels is the light that is coming from the magnificence of Jesus. That is the home that He is preparing for us.

In keeping with the same parallel of the bride and the bridegroom, Jesus promises a helper while He is away. "I will ask the Father, and He will give you another Helper, that He may be with you forever; that is the Spirit of truth, whom the world cannot receive, because it does not see Him or know Him, but you know Him because He abides with you and will be in you. 'I will not leave you as orphans; I will come to you. After a little while the world will no longer see Me, but you will see Me; because I live, you will live also'" (John 14:16–18). God has provided that helper the moment we believed. The moment we entered into this covenant relationship with Him, our spiritual eyes were opened and we were born again and received His divine nature. The Holy Spirit now seals us, empowers us, shapes us, molds us, leads us, guides us, and comforts us. He is our helper, our comforter, our friend that leads and guides and who protects us. It is amazing, absolutely amazing!

There is, however, a responsibility that we have as the bride. "Let us rejoice and be glad and give the glory to Him, for the marriage of the Lamb has come and His bride has made herself ready" (Rev. 19:7). We are the bride and we are called to make ourselves ready. We don't know when the bridegroom is returning. Scripture tells us no one knows the day or the hour of His return but we should know the season. I believe we are in that season. Are you ready? Have you prepared yourself? It's during this time when the bride prepares herself to learn how to love the bridegroom. What does love look like? For those of you who are married do you remember when you were courting your spouse? I remember the first time I looked into the eyes of my bride to be. I knew she was going to be mine, even though she was someone else's date. It was a double blind date and Jamie was my friend's date … lol The moment she opened the door and our eyes locked, I said, "That's the one." I knew it and she knew it. I remember my friend Steven was telling me he and Jamie were going to fall in love, get married and have kids, and I'd say nope, not happening," I knew it. Yes, he's forgiven me.

I can remember calling her on the phone and my heart pounding, "Wow, it's Jamie." I remember the anticipation of going to see her; I couldn't wait to see her and just hang with her. She's still the babe! I'm still enthralled with her, I still love hanging with her. Sometimes I even get mad at her because she is so busy with her work. I love being with her, talking to her, and listening to her. Sometimes I get accused of selective hearing, but that's okay… lol… In the same way Jesus is the lover of our souls and that is the kind of relationship He wants with you and me. It's not a one-sided thing, giving Him our list and checking it twice, making sure we are not naughty but nice. It is an abiding love relationship, the kind where you want to walk with Him and talk with Him, and again, it's not a sexual thing. It is a love so deep, so great, so more satisfying than that. It is a magnificent, beautiful walk that you could ever enjoy.

Paul says, "But I am afraid that, as the serpent deceived Eve by his craftiness, your minds will be led astray from the simplicity and purity of devotion to Christ" (2 Cor. 11:3). That is what the enemy is trying to do. He comes to steal, kill, and destroy. The enemy is so clever at directing our love to false lovers. Did you know busyness is a false lover? Shame, guilt, condemnation, they are all false lovers, and they are not even good lovers. Yet they direct our hearts away from our true love. Fear and anxiety, they are also false lovers. Lust is a false lover. These are all things the enemy uses to rob us of the deepest, abiding, union and communion with Christ. This is why in Revelation 2:4, when Jesus commended the church in Ephesus, He said they were doing some great things, they rejected false apostles and they hate the deeds of the Nicolaitans. You're doing pretty good things there, you're a strong church and are doing some things really well. But he also said, "I have this one thing against you, you left your first love." He didn't say you lost it, He said you left it, they found a false lover. That is the prophetic picture of Hosea the prophet and his wife the prostitute, Gomer. It is a prophetic picture of what happens when we turn to false lovers. We allow our love for Him to wane. When it is all said and done, "Love your God with all your heart, with all your soul, with all your mind, with all your strength."

There is another thing we must do as the bride; we must prepare ourselves: "The bride has made herself ready." "Be diligent to present yourself approved to God as a workman who does not need to be ashamed, accurately handling the word of truth" (2 Tim. 2:15). "All Scripture is inspired by God, profitable for teaching, reproof, correction, training and righteousness that the man of God may be adequately equipped for every good work" (2 Tim. 3:16). Just as the bride would learn the necessary skills to be a good wife, so also, the bride of Christ must learn the necessary skills to be a good bride for the Bridegroom. This means that not only do we need to know the Word of God, but we need to serve the Lord using the gifts, talents and abilities that He has given us. It is important because we are called to serve Him.

My love language is verbal affirmation and physical touch. Sometimes I'm like, "Jamie, I love you, I love you," and I want to touch her hair and rub her back. But sometimes Jamie says, "Chris, if you really loved me you'll do the dishes." Love is not an adjective; it's a verb. Most people don't know that. I didn't know that either. What do you think I do to demonstrate love? I do the dishes. Now I even cook. When she comes home from work, guess what happens? There is a meal on the table for her. She knows I love her and guess who benefits, I do. If you really love Jesus, you have to serve Him. Love is action.

There is a section in our membership packet at our church that says, "Every member is a minister and every minister has a ministry." We don't put that in just because we want people busy. Every one of us can serve God in some place. It could be being on the worship team, being in the sound booth, handling the camera, being on the prayer team, being on the power booth team, or in children ministries. There are so many places where a person could use their spiritual gifts and talents. It's like saying, "Papa, I'm making dinner for you tonight." You can't say I love you, I love you, I love you, but just don't tell me to do dishes."

There is another aspect of preparing yourself. Guys, can you imagine on your wedding day if your bride came in a beautiful white wedding dress after she walked through a coal mine. Imagine her walking down the aisle with soot all over her face. Or imagine your bride in that beautiful white dress, playing in the rain and making mud pies and she is walking down the aisle in a really dirty white dress. Imagine yourself as the bridegroom with great anticipation waiting for your bride to come and then you see her, "Whoa, something is not right here. That dress is really dirty, quick someone get her a new dress." I know that the moment you trusted Christ you were sanctified, glorified, and justified all at once, and yes, God no longer calls us a sinner. "But Scripture does say, shall we continue to sin so that grace may not abound, No, may it never be" (Rom. 6:1–2). God our Father says, "As obedient children do not fashion yourselves according to the former lusts of your ignorance but as He who has called you is holy, so be holy in all that you do" (1 Pet. 1:14). We are called to grow in grace from glory to glory. That is the preparation period. Yes, God called you and you are holy, but don't stay where you are at. Don't get stuck in all the bad habits that bind you. Repent and renounce your sins and take some steps forward. Sometimes, you will make a little mistake and you may go backwards, then confess it, repent of it and start stepping forward again (1 Jn. 1:9). If you mess up again or take a few steps backward, confess it, repent of it again start stepping forward again. You are making progress because you are no longer standing where you started. You are growing from glory to glory to glory. The bridegroom is coming. Are you ready for the bridegroom? He is looking is looking for a bride without spot and without blemish. We have to prepare. The bridegroom loves you and you are His favorite, just like me, so let's prepare.

CHAPTER 7

The Matan: The Bridal Gift

We have been learning how God used an ancient Jewish marriage ceremony to prophetically illustrate Christ the bridegroom and His bride the church. Every aspect of that ceremony is spiritually significant for us today. The same way Abraham had chosen a bride for his son Isaac, God has chosen a bride for His son, Jesus.

The Matan is the bridal gift and it is different from the bridal price. "When Abraham's servant heard their words, he bowed himself to the ground before the Lord. The servant brought out articles of silver and articles of gold, and garments, and gave them to Rebekah; *he also gave precious things to her brother and to her mother* (Gen. 24:52–53). Notice the servant gave gifts and he gave extravagantly. He gave far more than the bridal price. He gave articles of gold and silver to the brother, the mother and to the family. The bridal price was the price for the bride, the bridal gifts are to provide resources to bless the family.

Jesus paid the bridal price for our redemption but He also paid the bridal price for our gifts that He gives to each of us. "But to each one of us grace was given according to the measure of Christ's gift. Therefore it says,

"When He ascended on high,
He led captive a host of captives,
And He gave gifts to men" (Eph. 4:7–8).

The word *grace* is an interesting word and it has a dual meaning. On one hand it carries the idea of pardon (undeserved favor), and on the other hand, it carries the idea of His divine enablement or His energizing force of power. To each one of us in Christ, Jesus not only satisfied our sin debt and our bridal price, but also through His death, burial, and resurrection He purchased gifts. Simply said, the gifts of God cannot be earned and cannot be worked for. They are grace gifts, they are undeserved, these gifts are given as a gift.

If I want to give you a gift but I tell you in order to get it you have to work for it in my garden, is that a gift? No. It's no longer a gift; it's an obligation. Notice it says "to each one of us grace is given, in other words God has gifted each one of us not because we deserve it, not because we are brilliant, not because we are better than anyone else; He gives them sovereignly to each one of us according to His measure of His grace.

There are two kinds of gifts; there are the redemptive gifts and then the Charismata gifts that some call spiritual gifts. I don't like to call them spiritual gifts because all gifts are from the Holy Spirit, whether redemptive or Charismata. They are all provided for by the Spirit of God and by the sovereignty of God to whomever He wills.

The redemptive gifts: "For just as we have many members in one body and all the members do not have the same function, so we, who are many, are one body in Christ, and individually members one of another. Since we have gifts that differ according to the grace given to us, each of us is to exercise them accordingly: if prophecy, according to the proportion of his faith; if service, in his serving; or he who teaches, in his teaching; or he who exhorts, in his exhortation; he who gives, with liberality; he who leads, with diligence; he who shows mercy, with cheerfulness" (Romans 12:4–8). All of us are different members. Let me suggest to you that we are all shaped differently. Can you imagine if we were all shaped the same? That would be boring. Imagine if we were all preachers, you'd never leave service. We are all different, we are all shaped differently. Rick Warren uses the acrostic "SHAPE." First, All of us have been given *s*piritual gifts. Did you know you had spiritual gifts? Do you know what the purpose of spiritual gifts are for? They are given to you for others. Each one of us has been given them without exception if you know Christ. These spiritual gifts are given to be used.

The second thing, He has given you a *h*eart. This is your passion, your desire. Some may have a passion to serve young people, some may have a passion to serve little children, some may have a passion to serve those that are unfortunate or disabled in some way. Maybe some have a passion to serve adults, but all of us have that heart, the way that God has wired us.

"A" in the word "shape" is *a*bilities. God has given you special abilities, talents. Some of you may have the talent to play on the worship team, or work the sound booth, some have the ability to work with numbers, some can work with your hands and create and build. All of us have different talents and abilities. What are these talents and abilities for? They are for others, they are to be used.

The "P" in our outline is for *p*ersonality. All of us have different personalities. Some of you are extroverts like me, some of you are introverts. Some of you like to be in the front and some of you like to be in the background. This is because we have different personalities. God has wired us uniquely different.

The "E" in "shape" is for *e*xperience. That is life experience. Life has taught us certain things to do and not to do, how to avoid certain pit falls and how to navigate and cultivate relationships. These things are created by life experiences. All of us are from different backgrounds and different cultures. We grew up in different places and interacted with different people. This makes us unique. God has created a tapestry of His bride that is so uniquely different from one another but cultivated as one body.

Some of you have the ability to proclaim the Word of God, that is called prophecy in the redemptive gifts. Redemptive gifts are given to every person at salvation. Some of you have the ability to preach, some have the ability to teach, or have exhortation, which is the ability to warn and help people fulfill their destiny. Some may be able to give far beyond what others may give, whether it's your time, energy, resources, finances. Some have been called to lead and have been given that ability to lead people in the way God wants the body to go. Some have the gift of mercy, which is the ability to empathize with others. That is a precious gift because not everyone has the kind of patience to be able to empathize with those that are struggling.

There is another set of gifts I call the Charismata gifts. "Now there are varieties of gifts, but the same Spirit. And there are varieties of ministries, and the same Lord. There are varieties of effects, but the same God who works all things in all persons. But to each one is given the manifestation of the Spirit for the common good. For to one is given the word of wisdom through the Spirit, and to another the word of knowledge according to the same Spirit; to another faith by the same Spirit, and to another gifts of healing by the one Spirit, and to another the effecting of miracles, and to another prophecy, and to another the distinguishing of spirits, to another various kinds of tongues, and to another the interpretation of tongues. But one and the same Spirit works all these things, distributing to each one individually just as He wills" (1 Cor. 12:4–11). Again, it is being said that there is a variety of gifts. While everyone is given redemptive gifts Paul exhorts believers in 1 Cor. 12:31, "But earnestly desire the greater gifts."

Everyone is given the redemptive gifts at salvation, but then Scripture tells us there is more. The "more" that you get requires you to do something. The redemptive gifts are given sovereignly at salvation, you had no say in the matter, He just gave them to you. The greater gifts are the gifts that are acquired by an effort on your part to go after them. *Earnestly desire the greater gifts.* It requires an effort on your part to go after that which is greater.

There are a lot of churches that want to use white out in this passage of Scripture. They would say that this time (the time of greater gifts) is over. They may change their minds if they hang out at our church because we have seen so many miracles it's not even funny. The gift of healing is alive and well and many do not even know it. It is important to understand that all of the word of God is true. God is the same yesterday, today, and forever. He has not changed, His agenda is the same, He speaks today as He did to Abraham, He moved in the first century as He does today. God is a God of power, wonder, and glory. I believe a lot of these churches don't see anything happen because they do not realize there is more and they do not seek after what they do not know exists. If they do not seek that which they do not know exists, nothing is going to happen. The greater gifts require an effort from you to go after it.

Notice here, "And there are varieties of ministries, and the same Lord. There are *varieties of effects*, but the same God who works all things in all persons." What's the author talking about here, "effects"? He is talking about the manifestation of the Spirit of God on a person. Sometimes in the presence of God, you start weeping. Sometimes in the presence of God, the joy just overflows your heart and you begin to giggle. When I got baptized in the Holy Spirit I laughed and cried for almost 4 hours. Sometimes in the presence of God, His over whelming love comes over you like a blanket and you are just resting in a peace that is unexplainable. Sometimes, you are just resting in the love of God. There are different effects of the Holy Spirit when the Holy Spirit comes upon you. "But to each one is given the manifestation of the Spirit for the *common good*." The Holy Spirit brings blessing. You don't have to be afraid of the Holy Spirit. I know of a lot of pastors in our area that won't preach this because they are afraid something is going to happen. What do you think happened at Pentecost? That was crazy; they were accused of being drunk. Can you imagine that happening? I think that would be pretty cool personally. We should never be afraid of what God wants to do in our lives.

We, as children of God, should earnestly pursue the presence of God and earnestly pursue the gifts God wants us to have, because if there is anything we get from this, "There is more!" The Lord has given me a slew of gifts; He has given me words of knowledge, words of wisdom, tongues, interpretation of tongue, gifts of healings but you know what, there is more. I am not satisfied with where I am today. Yes, I have seen a lot of people healed when I lay hands on them; I'm thrilled by that. But there is more folks. I want to see the fullness of the kingdom of God in all of God's glory. I want to see the effecting of miracles, I want to see faith that moves mountains. I want to see the fullness of God come. Did you know that when Peter walked down the street, his shadow healed some people instantly, wholly smokes, that's anointing. I want it!

The God that we love is supernatural and He uses ordinary people to do extraordinary things. This is not something to be afraid of. It is something to embrace, because when God touches someone they would say, "Wait a minute, the devil can't heal anyone like this, then God must be real. That God is Jesus Christ who is the same yesterday, today, and forever. He can use you, He can use me, He can use every one of us. I don't know what redemptive gift you possess but let me ask you this, are you using it? Are you using the redemptive gifts God has given you? If not you are squandering something He has given you for the body of Christ. Are you pursuing the more? Or are you stuck in a place where you say you have all you need and all you want?

There are three categories of the Charismata gifts. Gifts of Knowledge: The Word of Wisdom, The Word of Knowledge and The Discerning of Spirits. Speaking gifts: Prophecy, Tongues and Interpretation of Tongues. Power gifts: The Gift of Faith, The Gifts of Healing and The Working of Miracles. Words of wisdom are given when God gives you special revelation for His purpose or circumstance in the life of other people. For example, maybe someone is going through a hard time and their life is entangled in a lot of messes and God gives you a supernatural revelation to untangle that mess, that is a word of wisdom. Then we have the word of knowledge, that is when God gives a revelatory word of a certain pain or a certain healing that needs to take place and it's always accompanied with the power gifts, specifically the gifts of healing. Then there is the distinguishing of spirits. It is the ability to see the supernatural and to understand a demonic source as opposed to a godly source. It is the ability to discern the difference between right and wrong, good and evil and the kingdom of darkness and the kingdom of light.

The second category of the Charismata gifts are the speaking gifts. This prophecy is different than the redemptive prophecy. The redemptive prophecy is forth telling the Word of God, proclaiming the Word of God much like I am doing right now. The Charismata prophecy is when God has given you a word to speak life into someone for a word of edification, exhortation and consolation. It is the ability to build them up and inspire them to walk into faith, it is calling them into their destiny. It is also foretelling. Sometimes it's telling a warning, "Watch out something is coming." It's foretelling, maybe it's calling you into a certain ministry or service. Then there is various types of tongues, notice the word various. Most are confused as far as tongues are concerned. When I was baptized in the Holy Spirit fifteen years ago, God gave me a private prayer language. This was my initial walk in the supernatural. I am praying in a language I don't understand and it's connecting me with God. It is a supernatural connection in which I am feeling His presence and I am speaking words, mysteries to Him that I don't even know (1 Cor. 14:2). It is divine connection and divine power in building up my inner man that is through tongues. Paul says, "I speak tongues more than you all and I wish you all spoke in tongues." If you don't speak in tongues, do it. It builds up the inner man. "But you, beloved, building yourselves up on your most holy faith, praying in the Holy Spirit" (Jude 1:20). Build yourself up; we are always called to build our faith. Prayer builds your faith; the word of God builds your faith. Praying in tongues builds your faith. There are also public tongues, sometimes it is a public tongue of praise, sometimes it is a public tongue of warfare; sometimes it is a public tongue of encouragement or a prophetic tongue. Public tongues must be interpreted where as private tongues is simply between you and God.

The third category of the Charismata gifts are the power gifts. Faith is the faith that moves mountains. There are different levels of faith; there is salvation faith, growing in faith, but then there is a kind of faith that is so supernatural that it is believing God to move mountains. I'll give you an example, I was at a Frontier Christian Fellowship event with the Royal Rangers years ago, the leader asked me nine months in advance if I would preach. I usually don't like taking these speaking engagements because I feel lead to preach at my home church. I said, "Skip, I'm sorry but …" As I was saying that God downloaded the entire message He wanted me to speak. I immediately told Skip I would go. The day is approaching and the whole week is supposed to be a complete washout. By Saturday night, we are supposed to have five inches of rain. By noon, it's dark. So I prayed, "Lord, you gave me a promise, you gave me this message, and I don't have a tent. If it rains I can't give this message. Lord, I'm asking right now that You keep the rain away." I then took authority over it. "In the name of Jesus, I command the rain not to rain over this place." It was extraordinary; I had never done this before. It's black outside, and it's only 5:00 PM, you could see the rolling thunder clouds. At seven o'clock, when I was about to speak, Skip comes running up to me and says, "Chris, you're never going to believe this. Look into the camera. I took pictures and there is this brilliant white radiance north, and there is a brilliant white radiance to the south and one to the east and another to the west." But you couldn't see it with the naked eye. However, the rain was pouring all around the camp but not in the camp. It was a torrential rain, but it wasn't raining in our camp. I got to speak and so many kids got touched by God like they never got touched by God before. That my friend is mountain-moving faith. There are also gifts of healing. Notice there is a plurality. There are various types of gifts of healing. It could be spiritual healing, emotional healing and physical healing. I want to see the day when I can see the dead raised, the lame walk, the blind see, the deaf hear. I want to see the day when I see limbs grow. There is testimony of this happening all over the world. I'm still operating in the gifts of healing, and I'm grateful for it but I want *more*! How do you get the more, you have to pursue. You get the "more" by earnestly desiring the greater gifts. You receive the greater gifts when you are pursuing God and His kingdom.

Now we are getting to another important part, stewardship. "As each one has received a special gift, employ it in serving one another as good stewards of the manifold grace of God" (1 Peter 4:10). If you are in Christ, you have received redemptive gifts. God has made you a steward, a manager. Remember we are talking about the Matan, just as Abraham gave the bridal gift to bless the family, God has given us spiritual gifts to bless the family of God. You are the family of God. They (the gifts) are given to you for others; they are not given to you to hide them, they are not given to you to sit on them. They are given to you for the benefit of the family of God so that the whole body builds one another up in the faith to become the measure and stature of the fullness of God. These gifts are given to you for others. It is a stewardship, meaning God has made you a manager of His resources. Isn't that amazing? God has entrusted you, with His resources to benefit the body.

What about activation? "Whoever speaks, is to do so as one who is speaking the utterances of God; whoever serves is to do so as one who is serving by the strength which God supplies; so that in all things God may be glorified through Jesus Christ, to whom belongs the glory and dominion forever and ever. Amen" (1 Peter 4:11). Here's the deal, how do you activate the gifts that have been given to you? Step out in faith. What if nothing happens? You keep doing it because it is not your responsibility it is His responsibility. "Whoever serves is to do so as one who is serving *by the strength which God supplies.*" The result is His problem. I am never afraid to pray for the sick. If nothing happens I just do it again, and again, and again. It is that stubbornness, that faith that activates the gift that has been given. Can you imagine praying for someone like this, "Oh, God, bring the right doctor, I hope it gets healed someday." Nothing happens and no wonder. Was that your best shot? No. Pray like this. "In the name of Jesus, I rebuke this pain, be healed in Jesus name!" Then you let God work through you. If it doesn't work you do it again, and again until it does. I tell people if you are not healed yet, just keep pursuing God because it is His promise. Be as stubborn as you possibly can because Scripture says, "By His stripes we are healed" (Isa. 53:5). That is a promise, and if I don't see it manifested, maybe there is an area in my life I need to work on and grow in. I am going to pursue it at all costs because I know it is a promise and it is true.

God not only gives the Charismata gifts sovereignly, but He also gives the Charismata gifts through Impartation. Paul says, "For I long to see you so that I may impart some spiritual gift to you, that you may be established" (Rom. 1:11) "Do not neglect the spiritual gift within you, which was bestowed on you through prophetic utterance with the laying on of hands by the presbytery" (1 Tim. 4:14). "For this reason I remind you to kindle afresh the gift of God which is in you through the laying on of my hands" (2 Tim. 1:6). These are three instances where impartation was given by the laying on of hands, but let me be clear, God is the one who is doing it. All we are is a jar of clay; we don't have any special power in and of ourselves. Yet we can become a channel of blessing used by the Holy Spirit.

I have discovered that when it comes to the Charismata gifts, you cannot lead where you have not been. You cannot teach what you do not know. You cannot give what you do not have. Look at the apostle Paul; he walked in signs and wonders. He was able to lead because he's been there. He was able to teach because he knew, he was able to impart because he had. That is why Jesus himself says, freely you have received, freely give. In other words, these gifts are for the body of Christ to be used for each other, whether they are redemptive gifts or Charismata gifts. They are all gifts of God for the glory of God for the benefit of His bride the church.

CHAPTER 8

The Bridegroom's Return

Remember, in the Jewish covenant of marriage, after the betrothal ceremony was over, the groom went away to build a house for his bride. That time was anywhere between nine months to a year. Once that home was approved by his father, the groom would return for his bride. What is fascinating, is that this was a planned, willful, kidnapping. She did not know the day or the hour of his return but she would wait expectantly, confidently and joyfully for his return. When he did return, he would snatch her up and take her to his bridal chamber in the new home he had prepared. They would stay in the bridal chamber seven days. On the seventh day, the Groom would introduce his wife to the dinner guests.

"Do not let your heart be troubled; believe in God, believe also in Me. In My Father's house are many dwelling places; if it were not so, I would have told you; for I go to prepare a place for you. If I go and prepare a place for you, I will come again and receive you to Myself, that where I am, there you may be also" (John 14:1–3). Forty days after Jesus was raised from the dead was the ascension. Jesus was lifted up into the heavens as the disciples are watching. It must have been amazing. Can you imagine being a disciple and watching Jesus literally being raised up to the clouds and staring in amazement and wonder as two angels show up and ask you, "Why you are staring into the sky?" Then they tell you, "This same Jesus you saw going into the sky will return the same way He left." That is really important. I want you to grab on to that; it's a promise. "In My Father's house are many dwelling places; if it were not so, I would have told you; *for I go to prepare a place for you.*" We've spoken about this place already; it's so amazing, so magnificent, so glorious, it is going to be so beautiful that we cannot comprehend it on this side of eternity. It is more amazing than we can possibly describe. That is not even the best part. The best part is that you would have an intimate union and communion with the Lord Jesus Christ forever.

The question I want to ask is this, what is this return and when will it happen? We often talk about the return of Christ in two events, the rapture of the church and the second coming of Christ. To be fair, the word *rapture* is not in your Bible. Did you know that? It is a theological word that comes from the Latin and means "to be caught up." It is a theological word that describes an event. Also, to be fair there are three major positions as to when this is going to take place. There are many people like myself, believe in a pre-tribulation rapture of the church which means that the rapture happens before the tribulation period and the second coming comes after the tribulation. There is also the pre-wrath position. M. Rosenthal, a Jewish believer who founded Zion's hope. He believes that the rapture is going to take place at the middle of the tribulation period. He also sees two events, he sees the rapture of the church at the middle part of the tribulation and he sees the second coming at the end of the tribulation period. There is a third position that is also very popular; it is the post-tribulation period. It is believed here that Christ is going to come at the end of the tribulation period but they see it as one event. Here, it is believed that the church will be raptured to meet the Lord up in the air and then the church comes back down to establish the millennial kingdom.

I believe more than anything else that the pre-tribulation rapture is the position that is most consistent with the Scriptures, certainly the only position that follows the model of the Jewish wedding covenant and that is the position I am going to present.

Let's go to a text that talks about what the rapture is, "But we do not want you to be uninformed, brethren, about those who are asleep, so that you will not grieve as do the rest who have no hope. For if we believe that Jesus died and rose again, even so God will bring with Him those who have fallen asleep in Jesus. For this we say to you by the word of the Lord, that we who are alive and remain until the coming of the Lord, will not precede those who have fallen asleep. For the Lord Himself will descend from heaven with a shout, with the voice of the archangel and with the trumpet of God, and the dead in Christ will rise first. Then we who are alive and remain will be caught up together with them in the clouds to meet the Lord in the air, and so we shall always be with the Lord. Therefore comfort one another with these words" (1 Th. 4:13–18).

The emphasis here is not to tell us the when the rapture takes place but to tell us what the rapture is. Apparently, what has happened during Paul's time is there were some Jewish believers that were teaching that if your loved ones in Christ had died they would not be resurrected; they would not see them again. This caused a great deal of grief among the body of Christ. Paul is saying, "Look, I don't want you to be ignorant or uniformed about those that have fallen asleep in Jesus. If you believe that Jesus died and rose again, your loved ones who are in Christ, they will be the first ones who rise. Then we who are alive and remain will be caught up with them in the clouds to meet the Lord in the air. This is important; I want you to hang on to this.

The rapture is this, believers both dead and alive, both Old and New Testament are being caught up from the earth to meet the Lord in the air, thus they will always be with the Lord. The only place we have even a smidgen of indication of when this is going to happen is with the phrase *"With the trumpet of God."*

The second instance where we see the rapture of the Church, "Behold, I tell you a mystery; we will not all sleep, but we will all be changed, in a moment, in the twinkling of an eye, at the last trumpet; for the trumpet will sound, and the dead will be raised imperishable, and we will be changed. For this perishable must put on the imperishable, and this mortal must put on immortality" (1 Cor. 15:51–53). In this passage of Scripture, Paul's emphasis is different than in 1 Thessalonians. 1 Thessalonians was dealing with what happens to the dead in Christ. The emphasis now is what happens to the body that is raised? Paul is clear that the body that is raised is raised imperishable. The mortal must put on immortality. In a moment, in a twinkling of an eye, the dead in Christ will receive their glorified body and we who are alive and remain will be translated into this same glorious body. By the way, this body will never stink of death or decay again; it will never face the limitations we face on this earth; your eyes will not go dim, your ears will not go deaf, you will not experience sickness, pain, or sorrow once you are caught up in the clouds to meet the Lord in the air. You will be completely, gloriously transformed with a new body.

Jesus also tells us one very important thing in Matthew's gospel. Jesus says that we will be like the angels; we will never be married or be given in marriage, we will never procreate again. Most of you are probably okay with that. Most post-tribulation believers believe that the last trumpet is the last trumpet of the judgments that are found in the book of Revelation called the trumpet judgments.

There are three series of judgments, the Seal judgments of which there are seven. There are the Trumpet judgments of which there are seven. And there are the Bowl judgments of which there are seven. The post-tribulation position believes that the last trumpet is the last trumpet judgment that signals the coming of Christ and it does, but I would say is the second event not the first event.

If the last trumpet judgment is not the trumpet blast that signals the rapture of the church, then we have to ask what is it? What is that trumpet? It cannot be the last trumpet in the trumpet judgments and here is why, let me give you several reasons. First, at the end of the tribulation, if the rapture of the church is one event then every believer of all time both dead and alive at the coming of the Lord, receive their glorified bodies and they enter the millennial kingdom.

Those that are raptured receive their glorified bodies and they can never procreate. Then you have to ask the question, who will repopulate the earth in the millennium? At the end of the millennial kingdom, in which the devil is bound for a thousand years, he will be loosed to deceive the nations once more. Then there is going to be the final war of Armageddon and the final separation of the sheep and the goats.

Who repopulates the millennial kingdom? To be fair, the post-tribulation believer would say that it would be the unbelievers that did not receive the mark of the beast. The Scriptures are clear, if you receive the mark of the beast, you are signed, sealed, and delivered for death forever. However, it is important to understand that an unbeliever regardless of whether he received the mark of the beast or not will still be judged and will not enter Christ's kingdom. Somebody has to repopulate the kingdom.

We are called rulers and co-reigners with Christ, are we not? If we enter the kingdom, and there are no subjects, who are we to rule over? Look at the destiny of the wicked at the end of the tribulation period. "But when the Son of Man comes in His glory, and all the angels with Him, then He will sit on His glorious throne. *All the nations will be gathered before Him; and He will separate them from one another, as the shepherd separates the sheep from the goats; and He will put the sheep on His right, and the goats on the left*" (Matt. 25:31–33). Now watch verse 46 where he is talking about the goats, "These will go away into eternal punishment, but the righteous into eternal life." The sheep and the goats are nothing more than a description of the righteous and the unrighteous. The sheep are represented by the righteous, those that have believed in Christ. The goats are represented by unbelievers. They are called wicked. At the end of the tribulation period, the angels come and they gather the elect and the nations that stand against Christ. There has been great devastation on the earth throughout this period, seal judgments, trumpet judgments, bowl judgments. Those that are left are standing before Christ are either sheep or goats, believers or unbelievers. There will be a great separation that will take place. Every unbeliever, without exception is cast into the lake of fire (Rev. 20:11–14). We see the Son of man coming clothed with a robe dipped in blood on a white horse and the sword that comes out of His mouth and He slays the wicked. Every unbeliever is described as the wicked ones, the ungodly ones, the goats that will not enter into the kingdom of God.

Who populates the kingdom if Christ comes at the end? Someone has to? Look at the wording of the two events.

1. Caught up from the Earth to the clouds
    "Then we who are alive and remain will be *caught up together with them in the clouds to meet the Lord in the air*, and so we shall always be with the Lord" (1 Th. 4:17).

2. Coming from Heaven to Earth
    He is clothed with a robe dipped in blood, and His name is called The Word of God. And the armies *which are in heaven*, clothed in fine linen, white and clean, were following Him on white horses (Rev. 19:13–14).

The rapture of the church is the gathering together, the catching up to be with Christ, to meet Him in the air and thus always be with the Lord. For the second coming, look at Revelation 19, "And the armies *which are in heaven*." The word *are* is in the present tense. They are not on earth. Remember the rapture is being caught up from the earth to the clouds. The second coming is coming from heaven to earth. See what it says next, "And the armies which are in heaven, *clothed in fine linen, white and clean*, were following Him on white horses. This is a reference that only refers to believers. These are the saints, the holy ones that have been washed by the blood of the lamb. They are wearing white robes and they are white and clean because the Lamb, the spotless, sinless Lamb of God has washed them clean by His blood. They are not angels. They are the saints that are celebrating in heaven during the seven years of tribulation that correlate to the seven days of celebration that we will see later.

If the last trumpet is not the last trumpet of the judgments, then what trumpet is it? This is an important question. This question has to be answered.

Did you know that the four feasts in the spring time revolve around Christ's death, burial, resurrection, ascension, and Pentecost when Holy Spirit comes? Did you know that Jesus actually died on the Day of Atonement? Do you know what the Day of Atonement is? In the Old Testament, the high priest would go into the Holy of Holies with a spotless lamb and he would slay it. He would then take a Hyssop plant and he would sprinkle the blood on the altar. This symbolized the once and for all sacrifice that Messiah would come to pay the penalty for our sins. The day of atonement was nothing more than a prophetic picture of what Christ would do. The four early feasts, the spring feasts center on those events.

What about the fall feasts? There are three fall feasts and holy days. Most theologians believe that is when Jesus is returning because the feasts represent what He is doing. Do you know what feast Jesus will come on? Rosh Hashanah, the feast of trumpets. It was during the feast of trumpets in the ancient times that the priests would start blowing the trumpets. As they blew these series of trumpets, it signaled the gathering of the saints for assembly.

No one knows the day or the hour but you should know the season. I know in my spirit that we are in the season. The trumpet blasts are not the judgments. Judgments are for the wicked. The trumpet judgments were judgments against the wicked. Those trumpet judgments are not for the redeemed. It is Rosh Hashanah, the feast of trumpets, that is for the redeemed, where they gather the people of God for assembly before the Lord. That is not even the most compelling reason why Christ is going to come before the tribulation period. The most compelling reason why Christ is coming before the tribulation period is because the Bible teaches that Christ's coming is imminent. It can happen at any moment. "For the grace of God has appeared, bringing salvation to all men, instructing us to deny ungodliness and worldly desires and to live sensibly, righteously and godly in the present age, *looking for the blessed hope and the appearing of the glory of our great God and Savior, Christ Jesus*" (Titus 2:11–13).

What are we supposed to be looking for? We are not looking for the tribulation period; we are not looking for the sign of the anti-Christ covenant with Israel; we are not looking for the Abomination of Desolation, we are not looking for any prophetic event except for Jesus. "My Bridegroom is coming, and I, the bride, need to be prepared." That is the exact picture we get in this Jewish wedding ceremony.

The picture in the wedding ceremony is that the bridegroom goes away and is building a home just as Jesus has promised us. Jesus promises to return. The bridegroom is coming but the bride is preparing herself for her bridegroom and she is waiting and anticipating and she is looking for her bridegroom to come. She is not looking for anything else. She is ready, she is holy, she is set apart with a beautiful, brilliant white dress, that is radiant and glorious.

"Therefore be patient, brethren, until the coming of the Lord. The farmer waits for the precious produce of the soil, being patient about it, until it gets the early and late rains. You too be patient; strengthen your hearts, for the coming of the Lord *is near*. Do not complain, brethren, against one another, so that you yourselves may not be judged; behold, the Judge *is standing right at the door*" (James 5:7–9). Every generation of believers, believed that they were in the season of Christ's return. Here is why, because in Matthew 24 we are told the signs of His coming will be war and rumors of war, there will be false Christs and pestilence and earthquakes. You will see these signs and wonders. When you see these signs, you will know the season is here. Every generation has had those signs. Think about the first generation. They saw the complete destruction of Jerusalem and the temple. Think about the Crusades. Think about the wars between Islam and Christianity. Think about the devastation that happened in Europe, Asia, and the Middle East. Think of WWI, the war to end all wars and WWII where over eighty million people were killed. That's a lot of death. Think about the pestilence, the black plague, bubonic plague, entire societies wiped out by pestilence. Go through any old cemetery and you will see little ones and old ones that died in the same year due to the same plague. Earthquakes have completely decimated entire cities. Every generation was longing and looking for Jesus. Every generation knew the coming of Christ was imminent. That means that Christ could come at any second. This is the whole reason for the parable of the young virgins to have their oil lamps trimmed. Be ready for the bride groom. "Now, little children, abide in Him, so that when He appears, we may have confidence and not shrink away from Him in shame at His coming" (1 John 2:28).

If you believe in a pre-wrath position, or if you believe in a post-tribulation position like many others, let me suggest to you that means that Christ's coming is not imminent, which contradicts Scripture. It means you are not looking for His coming but rather for the sign of the seven-year peace covenant between anti-Christ and Israel. Or it means you are looking for the temple to be rebuilt, because in the middle of the temple the anti-Christ is going to sit on the throne in the temple and declare himself to be God. Then you will be looking for the worldwide religion and worldwide economic system and the worldwide governmental system. You're looking for the time when the mark of the beast comes and you can't buy or sell without that mark. Then you are looking for the time when the saints would be beheaded for the testimony of Jesus and you're looking for that one time when anti-Christ breaks his covenant with Israel and comes against the nation of Israel with war. If you are not looking for the rapture, then you are looking for some other prophetic event if the rapture is not imminent.

Another reason for a pre-tribulational rapture is the reward. How shall we live? What do the Scriptures say? What is the bride's response? "For I am already being poured out as a drink offering, and the time of my departure has come. I have fought the good fight, I have finished the course, I have kept the faith; in the future there is laid up for me the crown of righteousness, which the Lord, the righteous Judge, will award to me on that day; and not only to me, but also to all who have *loved His appearing*" (1 Tim. 4:6–8). Here is Paul in the first century church, waiting, anticipating, and expecting Christ's return. He is ready, He is prepared. He is thinking that Jesus can come at any moment. Paul knows because of His faithfulness and his longing for Christ, because of his expectation for His return he is being rewarded with the crown of righteousness. This was back in the first century. Are you expecting him, are you anticipating His return? Are you longing for His return? Are you expecting Him to show up at any moment? Are you prepared for His return?

How do we respond? "You too be patient; strengthen your hearts, for the coming of the Lord is near" (James 5:8). Bride, be steadfast, be immovable, be strong in the grace that is in Christ Jesus. You the bride, be established in your heart. "Do not complain, brethren, against one another, so that you yourselves may not be judged; *behold, the Judge is standing right at the door*" (James 5:9). My father always said to me growing up, "Chris, when you point a finger at someone, three come back at you. Until you become perfect you have no right to point that finger." I am far from perfect and I have no right to point a finger at anyone. Grumbling comes because of pride, you can't be kind to people if you are full of pride, it is self-centeredness.

I've been praying that God turns the bride into powerful intercessors. I can't tell you how many people don't pray, they think it is boring. Prayer is our connection to our Bridegroom. We have the right and the privilege to experience the power of His presence as we enter into the Holy of Holies. We have the right to call upon our God asking Him to invade this rebel torn world with His power and grace.

There are two things God's people should be about. We should be people of worship and people of prayer. Ask yourself, are you a man or woman of prayer? I don't mean just sitting there thanking Him for your food, I'm glad you do that but I am talking about intercession. I'm talking about investing in the lives of people around you. I am talking about investing in the kingdom of God through your intercession, warring in the Spirit. I'm talking about breaking the kingdom of darkness because you have connected with God and you are powerfully moving heaven on earth.

Faithfulness in assembling together and encouraging one another is another way we need to respond. "Let us consider how to stimulate one another to love and good deeds, not forsaking our own assembling together, as is the habit of some, but encouraging one another; and all the more *as you see the day drawing near*" (Heb. 10:24–25). What day is near? The bridegroom is coming. That's the day we are looking for. We need to connect with Him and connect with each other. Our covenant relationships are what is going to help us, we need to connect and carry one another's burdens. This is why we have small groups and why we assemble. This is so important in the body because the enemy wants to isolate you. The enemy wants to bring you out of the flame because he knows that a coal that is brought out of the flame will always cool off. You cannot continue to keep a coal aflame by itself, it will always go out. We need each other.

Holy conduct and godliness, "Since all these things are to be destroyed in this way, what sort of people ought you to be in holy conduct and godliness" (2 Pet. 3:11). This is where the bride needs to grow and be mature and cast off the old man which is corrupt according to his deceitful desires to be made new in the attitude of the mind, to be a new man which is created in righteousness and holiness in truth (Eph. 4:22–24). Purity and Christ likeness; "When He is revealed, we shall be like him for we shall see Him as He is. Everyone who has this hope in him, purifies himself even as He is pure" (1 John 3:2–3). What hope? That He is going to appear and we will be like Him. That is the hope we have in Christ. Everyone who has this hope understands that it is a process of continually casting off the old man, putting to death the deeds of the flesh and to die to self every day. But it does not stop there. It is putting on the garment of Christ, being filled with His Spirit and living for Him. "He who loves his life will lose it and he who loses his life will save it." We have to stop resurrecting a dead corpse, that's the bottom line.

My friends, He's coming. Are you ready for the bridegroom, because He is coming. He is almost here. When I think that Jesus could come at any moment, it gets me so fired up. I am ready! That is the same picture that He gives us in this ancient Jewish marital covenant. The bridegroom goes away and He is building a home and He has to make it the best he knows how because his Papa has to approve it before He can get His bride. His bride is waiting and learning how to love her husband. She is waiting and she is watching. Nine months have passed, it could be any day now and then she sees him. Her heart becomes aflame because she is prepared. Are you prepared? Are you ready? The sheep will experience intimacy with God forever. The goats will hear, "Depart from me, I never knew you" and will be sent to the place set up for the devil and his fallen angels.

CHAPTER 9

The Marriage Supper

As we study the marriage supper of the Lamb, we are going to see more compelling reasons why during the tribulation the bride of Christ is in the wedding chamber in heaven during the greatest outpouring of wrath poured out on this earth. We are going to see all hell breaking loose on the earth and the bride in the wedding chamber in heaven with Christ. At the end of the tribulation period, the marriage supper of the Lamb will take place. You will see wedding guests that are invited to the marriage supper. These guests are the tribulation saints that come out of the tribulation as Jesus Christ announces His bride to His guests.

Let's go over the model again. The bridegroom and the bride in the ancient Jewish wedding ceremony exchange their covenantal vows in the betrothal ceremony. The deal is sealed with the sharing of the cup of wine. At this moment they are legally married. At this time, the bridegroom is not permitted to consummate the marriage. Instead, he goes away to build a home for his bride. When he goes away, he promises his bride that he will return. The bride will prepare herself for her coming bridegroom. She is going to learn how to love her husband and how to be a good wife. Even though she does not know the day or the hour of her bridegroom's return she does know the season. She knows it takes approximately nine to twelve months for her bridegroom to build a home for her. The closer she gets to that time period, she is waiting expectantly, she is waiting confidently, she is waiting patiently; but she is waiting and watching for the bridegroom to return.

According to Jewish tradition, when the bridegroom returns, he snatches her up. It is like a voluntary kidnapping. There is no announcement made. The bridegroom comes, grabs his bride and takes her to the wedding chamber where they stay for seven days. The imagery is staggering if you look at the comparison between Christ and His bride. As soon as they enter the marriage chamber, the bridegroom is going to have a friend who stands outside the wedding chamber and when the marriage is consummated he comes out and tells his friend who announces it to the wedding guests. Then they stay in that wedding chamber for seven days. At the end of the seven days the bridegroom and his wife emerge and then he announces his wife to the wedding guests. We will see this with Jesus and His bride.

Jesus at the last supper makes His covenantal vows. He says, "This is my body which is broken for you do this in remembrance of me. This is the cup of my blood, the cup of the new covenant, do this in remembrance of me." Then he shares the cup. At that moment, the deal is sealed. Jesus has announced that He is the bridegroom and He is paying the redemptive price for our salvation. Jesus is purchasing us from the slave market of sin so that we would be a holy bride set apart for Him. From eternity past, God had determined that He would have an acceptable bride for His worthy Son. Then Jesus paid the bridal price. After He died on the cross he was raised from the dead and walked among the disciples for forty days.

Jesus made a promise in John 14:2–3, he said, "In my father's house are many dwelling places if this was not so I would have told you for I go to prepare a place for you and if I go to prepare a place for you I will come and bring you to myself for where I am there you may be also." On the day of ascension Jesus ascended up into heaven, the disciples on the mountain watched Him go up into the clouds and they were bewildered and confused. Then two angels said, "Just as he ascended into heaven, He will return in the clouds." During this time, the betrothal period, it's called the Church Age. It is a time when the bride, called the church needs to wait patiently for the bridegroom's return, confidently and expectantly preparing herself for the bridegroom. One day at the last trumpet, not the last trumpet of judgment but at the last trumpet of Rosh Hashanah, the new year, the feast of trumpets, the dead in Christ shall rise and we who are alive and remain are caught up together in the clouds and meet the Lord in the air and thus we shall always be with the Lord. This is the snatching up where the Bridegroom snatches His bride from the earth and brings her to the bridal chamber, not seven days, but seven years.

Let's talk about what happens at the marriage supper of the Lamb. "Let us rejoice and be glad and give the glory to Him, for the marriage of the Lamb has come and His bride has made herself ready." It was given to her to clothe herself in fine linen, bright and clean; for the fine linen is the righteous acts of the saints. Then he said to me, "Write, 'Blessed are those who are invited to the marriage supper of the Lamb.'" And he said to me, 'These are true words of God'" (Rev. 1:7–9). In the model of the ancient Jewish ceremony of the wedding it is seven days. It is really fascinating that Daniel sees a vision of seventy weeks, and the seventieth week, without getting to deep, is called "The Time of Jacob's Trouble." In the New Testament, this is called the tribulation period. A week is seven days. This imagery of the seventy weeks is not seventy weeks but seventy years. The imagery of the seventieth week is not seven days but seven years. This time of Jacob's trouble in the Old Testament, is a seven-year tribulation that comes on the earth. In keeping with this imagery that God has given us of the bride and the bridegroom, the bride is brought into the wedding chamber not for seven days but for seven years. "For the marriage of the Lamb has come and His bride has made herself ready." Whether you believe in a pre-tribulation rapture or mid-tribulation rapture or if you believe in a post tribulation rapture of the church, we all agree that the marriage supper of the Lamb comes at the end of the tribulation period, without exception.

Here we have an announcement that was made. The bridegroom says that the time for the marriage supper of the Lamb has come; it's time to announce His bride the church. Who is the bridegroom? Jesus. Who is the bride? Us, the church. Now watch this, "It was given to her to clothe herself in fine linen, bright and clean; for the fine linen is the righteous acts of the saints." Let me suggest to you that the righteous acts of the saints is not self-righteousness. These are not righteous acts that you can do in your own strength and power. We are clothed with the righteousness of Jesus Christ by faith. "Therefore, having been justified by faith, we have peace with God through our Lord Jesus Christ" (Rom. 5:1). The word *justified* means "to be declared righteous." Therefore, the righteous acts of the saints are acts that are done in the name of Christ, by the power of the Holy Spirit for the glory of God. Scripture is absolutely clear that apart from Him we can do nothing. You cannot, I cannot, perform any righteous act in our own strength, wisdom, or power. Every righteous act that we do is done in the name of Jesus Christ, by the power of the Holy Spirit, for the glory of God. The bride has made herself ready. How has the bride made herself ready? The bride has made herself ready by the righteous acts, by faith in Jesus Christ, doing the acts of faith, in the name of Christ by the power of the Holy Spirit for the glory of Christ. We are prepared for the coming of the bridegroom, when we learn to serve the bridegroom with the resources he has already given us. We've talked about this before. The Holy Spirit has given us gifts, He has given us talents and abilities, and has given us spiritual gifts for what purpose? To serve God and others with the talents and abilities He has given to us. As we serve one another in the name of Christ, by the power of the Holy Spirit for the Glory of Christ, the church is built up into the unity of the faith in the measure and the stature of the fullness of God. It is during that time that the bride makes herself ready. It means that God did not save you to do nothing. God has saved you for a divine purpose. He has saved you to serve Him by serving others. That's our preparation period for the bridegroom's return.

Next, look at that, "'Blessed are those who are invited to the marriage supper of the Lamb'. And he said to me, 'These are true words of God.'" As I stated before, the bridegroom is Jesus, the bride is us, the church. Let me suggest to you that you don't invite the bridegroom and the bride to the wedding feast. They are the ones being honored. This is important, you do not invite the bride or the bridegroom to the wedding feast because they are the ones being honored. The dinner is held in their honor. We then have to ask this question, who are the wedding guests? That's the question that we have to answer.

Jesus gave us a parable identifying who these people are. Scripture is wonderful in interpreting Scripture by Scripture. "The kingdom of heaven may be compared to a king who gave a wedding feast for his son. And he sent out his slaves to call those who had been invited to the wedding feast, and they were unwilling to come. Again, he sent out other slaves saying, 'Tell those who have been invited, "Behold, I have prepared my dinner; my oxen and my fattened livestock are all butchered and everything is ready; come to the wedding feast."' But they paid no attention and went their way, one to his own farm, another to his business, and the rest seized his slaves and mistreated them and killed them. But the king was enraged, and he sent his armies and destroyed those murderers and set their city on fire. Then he said to his slaves, 'The wedding is ready, but those who were invited were not worthy. Go, therefore to the main highways, and as many as you find there, invite to the wedding feast.' Those slaves went out into the streets and gathered together all they found, both evil and good; and the wedding hall was filled with dinner guests. "But when the king came in to look over the dinner guests, he saw a man there who was not dressed in wedding clothes, and he said to him, 'Friend, how did you come in here without wedding clothes?' And the man was speechless. Then the king said to the servants, 'Bind him hand and foot, and throw him into the outer darkness; in that place there will be weeping and gnashing of teeth'" (Matt. 22:2–13). In this parable Jesus is bringing us back to this analogy of Christ the bridegroom and His bride the church. He is saying the kingdom of God is compared to the king. Who is the king? The Father. The Father had determined from eternity past that he would find an acceptable bride for His worthy Son. Who are the slaves in this parable? Slave is a word we often interchange with the word servant. Who are these servants? The guests are the believers that are saved during the tribulation period. The servants that witness are those that God has called to be the evangelists during that time period. We know that there are two specifically mentioned called the two witnesses that were also prophets who also spoke powerfully to the nation of Israel. And we can surmise that God has raised up other servants in order to evangelize. Here we are in the tribulation period and God is calling the servants to go to national Israel, but national Israel has once again rejected Messiah. But God in His mercy according to Revelation chapter 7, in spite of Israel's rejection of Messiah and the acceptance of anti-Christ, will save twelve thousand from each of the twelve tribes of Israel. Then the anti-Christ will sit on the throne in the temple declaring himself to be god in an event called the Abomination of Desolation. It is tragic that national Israel will accept the anti-Christ as god and reject Jesus Christ, their true Messiah. But God in His mercy will save 144,000 Jewish people, twelve thousand from every tribe. Right now there are six million Jews in Israel and only 144,000 are sealed during this time because the nation of Israel has rejected Messiah again.

In Revelation 19, Jesus Christ, who is sitting on a white stallion, clothed in brilliant array is coming with the sword in His mouth and He is going to slay the wicked. He has an army of saints following Him wearing white clothes, riding horses, that is His army. It is at the end of the Tribulation period that Christ and His army will come out of heaven. They are going to come and there will be a sifting that takes place, on the left side will be the goats and on the right side will be the sheep. It is a reference to the unbeliever who has rejected Messiah and the believer who has accepted Messiah.

"Then the king said to the servants, 'Bind him hand and foot, and throw him into the outer darkness; in that place there will be weeping and gnashing of teeth.'" During the tribulation period, God sends His servants to bring the gospel to the lost. God specifically raised up these servants that are going to go and bring the gospel first to the house of Israel even though the nation of Israel is going to reject Messiah. In the mercy of God, twelve thousand from every tribe are going to be sealed and then God sends other servants to the nations. Revelation 7 says, "People will be saved from every nation, every tribe, every tongue, every language. It will be the greatest revival that this world has ever seen. The bride of Christ during this time is in the bridal chamber (heaven). At the end of the tribulation period, after all of hell is breaking loose on the earth, those still alive were ushered into the presence of Jesus Christ who comes back from heaven with His bride, the church, the armies of God." That is when He introduces His wife to these guests at this wedding feast. Who are the guests of the wedding feast? They are those that come out of the tribulation period that have not yet received a glorified body. When the church is raptured, they receive a glorified body, they can never marry or be given in marriage and at the end of the tribulation period every wicked soul that has rejected Messiah will be sent to the place called the lake of fire. There is no escape. There is only one shot that they have and that is to trust Jesus Christ while they have breath. The bridegroom comes with His bride as He introduces her to His dinner guests, the tribulation saints.

Remember, the millennial kingdom must be repopulated again. The believer, the bride does not repopulate the earth. They are like the angels who neither marry nor are given in marriage. The kingdom can only be populated by these dinner guests that have come to celebrate the marriage supper of the Lamb. They come to celebrate Christ the bridegroom and His bride the church.

If the bride is in the wedding chamber during the tribulation period, we should see some evidence of that. Let me show you an outline of future events. "When I (John) saw Him, I fell at His feet like a dead man. And He placed His right hand on me, saying, "Do not be afraid; I am the first and the last, and the living One; and I was dead, and behold, I am alive forevermore, and I have the keys of death and of Hades. *Therefore write the things which you have seen, and the things which are, and the things which will take place after these things*" (Rev. 1:17–19). This is a threefold outline on the entire book of revelation.

- Therefore write the things which you have *seen* (past),
- the things that *are* (present),
- the things which will take *place after these things* (future).

Jesus gives this outline in the book of Revelation, past, present, and future:

Now we are going to look at the things that are past. "Therefore write the things which you have *seen*." The things that he is writing about that he has seen is the vision He has of Jesus in chapter 1 of Revelation, this is the first part of the outline.

Next, "the things which are" (present) "'Write in a book what you see, and send it to the seven churches: to Ephesus and to Smyrna and to Pergamum and to Thyatira and to Sardis and to Philadelphia and to Laodicea'" (Rev. 1:11). These letters to these churches are mentioned in chapter 2 and chapter 3. The things that are present are the letters to the 7 churches. Some suggest that these letters to the seven churches are only letters specific to these seven in Asia minor. Let me suggest to you that these letters are not written just for these churches but for every church in every geographical area, in every time period. There is a key to understanding this passage.

Let's talk about the different churches. The letters are letters of correction and commendation and also a letter calling for repentance. Ephesus was the church that left its first love, and they were called to repent. Smyrna was the persecuted church. This was a church that was going through great tribulation, it was a church that many were being killed and Jesus says to them, "Hold fast to what I have promised you" even in the midst of awful persecution. Pergamum was the rebellious church. Thyatira was the immoral church, Sardis was the dead church, Philadelphia was the church that had little power but kept His word, Laodicea was the lukewarm church.

These commendations and corrections are not just for these specific churches, but these corrections and commendations reflect the kind of believers that are in the world in every age, in every time period, in every geographical location and even today. There are some believers like Ephesus that have literally left their first love. These letters speak today as they did in those days. There are some churches and believers like Smyrna that are being persecuted, some are being beheaded and crucified today. More people have been killed for their faith in the last one hundred years than in the last two thousand put together. There are some believers and churches like Pergamum that are plain rebellious. There are some churches and believers like Thyatira that are immoral. We are living in the most immoral age on the planet in its history. There are believers and churches like Sardis that resemble nothing more than a corpse, they are dead. We have been called to celebrate. We are living instruments of praise and worship for Him. There are some churches like Philadelphia that have little power but keep His word. This is a large part of the church body they hold to a form of godliness but deny it's power. There are some believers and some churches like Laodicea that are lukewarm. But that is not the key to understanding this passage. These letters apply to every age, in every geographical location, of every believer.

The key to understanding this passage is in these words "he who overcomes." The person who wrote first the epistle of 1 John is the same person that wrote the book of Revelation. "For whatever is born of God *overcomes* the world; and this is the victory that has *overcome* the world—our faith. Who is the one who *overcomes* the world, but he who believes that Jesus is the Son of God? (1 John 5:4–5). Who is the overcomer? We are the over comers because we have been born again, we have received, God's divine nature, we have been sealed by the Holy Spirit as promised, we are the bride of Christ we are the overcomers, we are signed, sealed, and delivered, baby!

Now, I'm not going to mention all the seven churches, I'll just mentioned some and you'll get the idea. To Thyatira he says, "He who *overcomes*, and he who keeps My deeds until the end, *to him I will give authority over the nations;* and he shall rule them with a rod of iron, as the vessels of the potter are broken to pieces, as I also have received authority from My Father" (Rev. 2:26–7). To Sardis, "He who *overcomes* will thus be clothed in white *garments*; and I will not erase his name from the book of life, and I will confess his name before My Father and before His angels. He who has an ear, let him hear what the Spirit says to the churches'"(Rev. 3:5–7). Every letter ends with "He who overcomes." These letters are applicable to every believer in every generation and in every geographical location who confesses the name of Christ.

What is given to the overcomer?" *I will give authority over the nations;* [27]and he shall **rule** them with a rod of iron, as the vessels of the potter are broken to pieces, as I also have received authority from My Father." Look at Sardis, "He who *overcomes*, thus will be clothed in white garments." We saw white garments with the bride didn't we? We saw that the bride was clothed with white linen bright and clean which was the righteousness acts of the saints. Laodicea, "He who *overcomes*, I will grant to him to sit down with Me on My throne, as I also overcame and sat down with My Father on His throne" (Rev. 3:21).

Just in these three churches we have several things, to one, He will grant authority and they would rule nations, they would sit on thrones, they will wear white garments. In the book of 1 Corinthians you will discover you will also receive crowns. Some will receive the crown of righteousness for loving His appearing. For elders who rule with honor and dignity will receive the crown of glory. Every believer will receive the incorruptible crown; we will receive the crown for faithful service for acts that are done in the name of Jesus Christ, in the power of the Holy Spirit for the glory of Christ. We will be given rewards.

Now remember we have to find if the bride is in the wedding chamber during the tribulation period. We already looked at things past and present. Now look at this. *"After these things* I looked, and behold, a door standing open in heaven, and the first voice which I had heard, like the sound of a trumpet speaking with me, said, 'Come up here, and I will show you *what must take place after these things'"* (Rev. 4:1). This verse starts out "After these things," what things? After the church age. "Around the throne were twenty-four thrones; and upon the thrones I saw twenty-four elders sitting, clothed in white garments, and golden crowns on their heads" (Rev. 4:4). What do elders do? Elders rule. This is the first time in the entire Bible where you will see an elder in heaven. After this verse, you see these elders mentioned twelve more times throughout this tribulation period.

The reason why the book of Revelation is difficult to understand is because it uses a lot of symbols. Here we have a symbol, that symbol is twenty-four elders. Let me suggest that there is a reason why he sees twenty-four. I believe that it is symbolic of the entire bride of Christ. Twenty four, twelve tribes of Israel and twelve apostles representing the entire bride of Christ from the Old Covenant and the New Covenant. They are on thrones, wearing white garments, with golden crowns on their heads. These are not angels, these are saints. What we have here is a description. John doesn't come out and say it is the bride but he tells us by description who these people are. The twenty-four is representative of the Old Covenant saints and the New Covenant saints that have been raptured up and they are in the bridal chamber. You see them throughout the book of revelation worshipping the Lamb along with the angels.

Now back to the marriage supper of the Lamb, "Let us rejoice and be glad and give the glory to Him, for the marriage of the Lamb has come and His bride has made herself ready." It was given to her to clothe herself in fine linen, bright and clean; *for the fine linen is the righteous acts of the saints.* Then he said to me, "Write, 'Blessed are those who are invited to the marriage supper of the Lamb.'" And he said to me, "These are true words of God" (Rev. 19:7–9). Here is what is taking place. The bridegroom, Messiah has snatched up his bride and has brought her to the wedding chamber. It is there, in the wedding chamber where the bride is wearing white robes with golden crowns on their heads and they are sitting on thrones with the Lord. They are ready and prepared to rule and reign with Him in the millennial kingdom. God is sending out His servants during this hellish time on earth to bring the gospel to all the nations and he starts with Israel first. But tragically, the nation of Israel has rejected the true Messiah and have embraced the anti-Christ in what is described as the abomination of desolation. This is when anti-Christ takes a seat on the throne in the rebuilt temple and declares himself god. But God in His mercy saves 144,000 Jewish people, twelve thousand from every tribe. Then God sends servants to the nations where the gospel is brought to every nation and tribe. Then they are gathered together at the end of the tribulation and there is a sifting that takes place when the bridegroom comes with His bride to establish His millennial rule on earth.

As Jesus, the bridegroom, announces His bride, the wedding guests are assembled. All of a sudden, Messiah is going to see some that do not have the proper clothing and that proper clothing is the righteousness that comes by faith in Jesus Christ. They are wearing the wrong clothing. They thought that they could enter in by being just a good person, but their goodness just doesn't cut it. All of our righteousness are like filthy rags. There is a further sifting that takes place. The goats go to the left, the sheep to the right. The sheep enter into the marriage supper of the Lamb where they celebrate the wedding feast between the Son of God and his bride the church.

We have to prepare ourselves for the bridegroom's return. He is coming at any moment, and His coming is imminent. Are you ready, are you prepared? There are two ways you can prepare; if you haven't accepted Christ as your Savior I want you to encourage you to do that today. You cannot wait; the only acceptable time for salvation is now. If you are a believer reading this today, just know, God has a divine destiny for you. Every one of you has a calling on your life to serve the King. He has given you a heart, spiritual gifts and abilities. Some of you understand technology, some of you are teachers, some of you can play instruments and some of you can sing, some can help. Every believer is a minister in God's kingdom. Every one of us has to find a place to serve. That's how we prepare, we prepare by growing in sanctification and by serving the king. You should have at least one ministry, prayer team, sound both, children's ministry, small groups, whatever it is. There has got to be a place that you are wired, that you can fit. We don't do that because God needs us, that's not why we do this. We do this because God has designed us for this; he has wired us for this. This is nothing more than preparation time. We have to be ready!

Let me just say this, no matter what He loves you. There is therefore no condemnation to those that are in Christ Jesus (Rom. 8:1). Praise God for that. He loves us with an everlasting love and He says this, "I know the plans that I have for you declares the Lord, plans to prosper you and not to harm you, plans for a hope and a future" (Jer. 29:11). His banner over us at all times is love. He won't condemn you no matter what you do, but there is one who will and that is the devil. If you want the blessings of the King you have to seek first God's kingdom. His love is unconditional and extravagant but His favor is on those that seek Him. His love for you is extravagant, you can't disappoint Him, He can't even get mad at you because He is only filled with love for you. But if you want His favor, remember this verse, "And Jesus kept increasing in wisdom and stature and grew in favor with God and men" (Luke 2:52). If Jesus had to grow in favor with God I think we do also. The way you grow in favor is by walking with the King in light of His kingdom. We are called to be Kingdom saints with an upward focus and when we do that we will grow in favor with God and with man.

CHAPTER 10

Co-Reigning

Once again, according to the model of the ancient Jewish wedding ceremony we will see a correlation between a husband and wife co-reigning in their household and Christ and His bride co-reigning in His kingdom.

We also are going to see a further difference between the rapture of the church which is "a snatching up" of the bride and the bride coming down out of heaven. "And I saw heaven opened, and behold, a white horse, and He who sat on it is called faithful and true, and in righteousness, He judges and wages war. His eyes are a flame of fire, and on His head are many diadems; and He has a name written on Him, which no one knows except Himself. He is clothed with a robe dipped in blood, and His name is called the Word of God. *And the armies which are in heaven, clothed in fine linen, white and clean, were following Him on white horses.* From His mouth comes a sharp sword, so that with it He may strike down the nations, and He will rule them with a rod of iron; and He treads the wine press of the fierce wrath of God, the Almighty. And on His robe and on His thigh He has a name written, 'KING OF KINGS, AND LORD OF LORDS'" (Rev. 19:11–16).

The bride has been snatched up, the bride is in the bridal chamber, which is in heaven during the seven-year period. Then at the end of the tribulation period something happens, John sees heaven open. Picture a door open and you are able to see inside the door and what He sees is absolutely astounding. He sees the glory and the majesty of Jesus Christ, the King of Kings and Lord of Lords, His eyes are like flames of fire. On His head are many diadems. He has a robe dipped in blood, which speaks of the nature of His sacrifice, as the lamb of God that came to take away the sins of the world. The blood is the picture of the redemptive work of Christ. He satisfied the wrath of God on our behalf. Wow! This door is open and he sees this majestic white stallion. The glory of the majestic King coming out of heaven down to earth.

This is a different picture from the rapture of the church. The word rapture as we mentioned earlier in the book is a theological word, which means "to snatch up." The rapture is the bride being snatched up from the earth to meet the Lord in the air, and thus we will always be with the Lord. However, in the verses just read, we have a picture of heaven opened and the King of Kings coming out of heaven. Notice also there are others following Him. The armies clothed in fine linen, white and clean were following Him on white horses. The fine linen, white and clean is clearly stated in Scripture, that this is the righteous act of the saints. It's not our own righteousness, it is the righteousness that has been imputed to us, reckoned to our account through faith in Jesus. These acts are done in the name of Christ by the power of the Holy Spirit for the glory of God. This is a picture of the bride who are also riding on white horses. They are clothed in holy array, as John is looking into heaven he sees Christ coming out and the armies of heaven coming out. According to Matthew 22, they come with one purpose, that is, to establish the millennial rule of Jesus Christ in which they will be sitting on thrones wearing crowns. They will be ruling and reigning with Him in perfect righteousness. It's amazing, what a privilege, the authority to co-reign with Christ.

As I studied this ancient Jewish ceremony, I found that according to Jewish tradition when a Jewish man married a Jewish woman they believed they literally became one soul. In Jewish tradition, a man is not complete until he gets married. Singleness is considered, by a man, not to be complete. When they do marry and are united together they co-reign in the household with the woman having equal authority over her children with the husband as the head and final authority over all decisions. Just like Christ and His bride the church. We have the privilege to sit on thrones with the King of Kings. We have the privilege to reign with Him in perfect righteousness. You won't even make a bad decision.

Watch what takes place here in this prophetic timeline. "Then I saw an angel coming down from heaven, holding the key of the abyss and a great chain in his hand. And he laid hold of the dragon, the serpent of old, who is the devil and Satan, and bound him for a thousand years; and he threw him into the abyss, and shut it and sealed it over him, so that he would not deceive the nations any longer, until the thousand years were completed; after these things he must be released for a short time" (Rev. 20:1–3). What takes place here is that the bride of Christ follows the King of kings down to earth, the sheep and the goats are separated. Those that trusted Christ, the true Messiah during the tribulation will go to the marriage supper of the Lamb, and it is they that are ushered into the kingdom. It is during that time that they, the believers that were saved in the tribulation period, they will repopulate the earth, they will marry and be given in marriage. The bride of Christ will rule and reign. But something also takes place here, and that is, Satan is bound, he is chained. The reason he is chained is because Christ is going to reign with His bride in perfect righteousness, the enemy the devil, will not have the ability to deceive the nations for the thousand years.

I find it amazing that there are some that are teaching that Satan is bound today. They are saying that the kingdom of God is amillenial. They are basically saying that it is a spiritual kingdom not a physical kingdom and yet what they haven't realized is that this is the Davidic covenant being restored. There will be a literal, physical kingdom in which the bride of Christ rules and reigns and Satan is bound during that time, not this time. How do we know this? Scripture says in 2 Corinthians 11:3, "But I am afraid that just as the serpent deceived Eve by his craftiness, that your hearts may be lead astray from the simplicity and the purity of your devotion to Christ." Right now, the devil is deceiving people. Someday he will be bound, so that he will not be able to deceive people. Think of 1 Peter 5:8 "Be of sober spirit, be on the alert. *Your adversary, the devil*, prowls around like a roaring lion, seeking someone to devour." Ephesians 6:12 says, "For our struggle is not against flesh and blood, but against the rulers, against the powers, against the world forces of this darkness, against the spiritual forces of wickedness in heavenly places." My friend, it's getting pretty dark out there. We do have an enemy and he is real. But we have all the authority we need to defeat the kingdom of darkness. We have everything we need pertaining to life and godliness through the knowledge of Him who called us to His own glory and excellence.

We don't have to be afraid of the kingdom of darkness because we have authority. There is a sense in which we rule even now. We are seated with Christ in the heavenly places (Eph. 2:6). Where? "Far above all rule and authority, power and dominion and over every name that is named not only in this age but in the age to come" (Eph. 1:20–21). Not only now but later. We have the authority to rule and reign over the kingdom of darkness. "Then I saw thrones, and they sat on them, and judgment was given to them. And I saw the souls of those who had been beheaded because of their testimony of Jesus and because of the word of God, and those who had not worshiped the beast or his image, and had not received the mark on their forehead and on their hand; and they came to life and reigned with Christ for a thousand years. The rest of the dead did not come to life until the thousand years were completed. This is the first resurrection. Blessed and holy is the one who has a part in the first resurrection; over these the second death has no power, but they will be priests of God and of Christ and will reign with Him for a thousand years (Rev. 20:4–6).

Here we see two resurrections, a resurrection of life and a resurrection of death. God in His mercy resurrects these souls that had been beheaded during the tribulation period. He resurrects those because they had not received the mark of the beast and because they had embraced Jesus the Messiah. These believers were martyred for their faith and Jesus resurrects them so that they also will rule and reign in the millennial kingdom. They will receive a glorified body just like the bride the church. They will co-reign with us. Notice this phrase, "This is the first resurrection." That is the resurrection of life; that is the first resurrection. There are two resurrections, the resurrection of life and the resurrection of death. We know there are multiple resurrections of life, Jesus was the first fruit of the resurrection, was He not? Then we know there is the rapture of the church, when the dead in Christ have risen. We who are alive will be translated and brought up, caught up to the clouds to meet the Lord in the air. As just stated, that even here is the resurrection of the saints that went through the tribulation period, that were martyred. That is the third resurrection of the resurrection of life. Then we know that after the thousand years are completed those believers that came out of the tribulation into the kingdom that were married and given in marriage and have died will be resurrected. Remember, they had not received their glorified body as of yet, and they also had died during that time. They will be resurrected at the end of the thousand years. That's the resurrection of life, the resurrection of that kind.

But there is also a resurrection of death. This is what should motivate every believer in Jesus Christ to share the message of truth of the gospel of our salvation. In the following verses we see the resurrection of death. "Then I saw a great white throne and Him who sat upon it, from whose presence earth and heaven fled away, and no place was found for them. And I saw the dead, the great and the small, standing before the throne, and books were opened; and another book was opened, which is the book of life; and the dead were judged from the things which were written in the books, according to their deeds. And the sea gave up the dead which were in it, and death and Hades gave up the dead which were in them; and they were judged, every one of them according to their deeds. Then death and Hades were thrown into the lake of fire. *This is the second death, the lake of fire.* And if anyone's name was not found written in the book of life, he was thrown into the lake of fire" (Rev. 20:11–15).

There are several resurrections of life and then the resurrection of death, which there is one. It is the final sending off every unbeliever that has rejected Messiah. It is final, it is eternal, and it is torturous. Think about this, every moment someone is dying today, every time I snap my fingers, someone has passed into eternity without hope. Snap, another soul is gone, loved ones, friends, relatives, countrymen, from all the nations are passing into eternity every moment and it's forever, forever. It is horrible!

I don't know if you ever read Dante's inferno where he described the different levels of hell. But if that doesn't motivate us, the love of Christ will. Paul says, "The love of Christ compels me to share the gospel" (2 Cor. 5:14). We have been given authority to rule and reign now. Jesus said, "All authority in heaven and earth has been given to me, now go" (Mt. 28:18). It is not a gospel empowered by words only, it is not a gospel that speaks and give moral arguments about different theologies. It is a gospel of power.

Jesus commissions twelve disciples who became apostles. He said to them, "Go, proclaim the kingdom of God, heal the sick, cast out demons." He gave them His authority to do His work, to represent Him. And these disciples went two by two, proclaiming the kingdom of God, they healed the sick and they cast out demons. They exercised the power and authority that Jesus gave them. In Luke chapter 10, Jesus commissioned seventy unnamed disciples with the same authority. They were commissioned to proclaim the kingdom of God, heal the sick, and cast out demons. And they return and said, "Lord, even the demons are subject to your name." Remember, this was even before the New Covenant, before we the church were permanently indwelt and empowered by the Holy Spirit. In Mark 16:15, it says, "Preach the gospel to all nations and these signs will follow those who believe, in my name they will cast out demons, they will speak in new tongues, they will lay hands on the sick and they will recover." When Jesus commissioned His disciples, He didn't say, "Pray for the sick." He said, "Heal the sick." Heal them, take authority over sickness and disease. We don't even realize the power that is available to us: "The surpassing greatness of His power to us who believe" (Eph. 1:19).

Do you realize that the authority God has given us is first and foremost the authority to shepherd our souls? We have the authority to say, "Flesh, I command you to die in Jesus name, that is not who I am. I am not an adulterer, I am not a gossiper, I am not bitter, I am not who the devil wants me to be. That is not who I am. I bind that tormenting, tempting spirit that's harassing me right now. Leave! In Jesus Name." We have authority over our soul. "Submit therefore to God. Resist the devil and he will flee from you" (Jas. 4:7).

We have authority over the kingdom darkness. Those lying spirits are constantly tempting, seducing, tormenting. Why don't you just exercise the authority God gave you! Resist the devil and he will flee! I get so ticked off at the enemy that I want to beat the snot out of him, not him beat the snot out of me. Let's learn to wreck his day; he'll go bother someone else won't he? He smartens up real quick because he is a bully. You know what a bully is? A bully is someone who picks on someone who he knows he can get over on. That's what a bully is. If you smack a bully in the nose they are no longer a bully, they whimper away. That is what the enemy is, nothing more than a bully lying to us all the time. You have authority now. You don't have to wait until we get to the kingdom to rule and reign. You have the authority to speak into each other's lives. You have the authority to break off that which is hindering your brother or sister who is weak. We have to rise up in these last days, because when it gets dark, the light has to get brighter. We are not wimpy people. We are a people who are so powerful that we have yet to tap in to the fullness of Him. And when we do, we are setting the kingdom of darkness on notice. I'm coming after it. That's how we expand the kingdom of God.

Folks, the church has to be the church. I can't tell you how many people are walking out there not knowing who they are or whose they are. Let that not be us. We are the bride, we co-reign, we are seated with Christ in heavenly places. We have been given a measure of His authority in the name of Christ, that name is the Name that is above all Names. "At the name of Jesus, every knee shall bow in heaven and in earth and under the earth, every tongue will confess that Jesus Christ is Lord" (Phil. 2:10–11). So let us proclaim the Name of Jesus Christ for the glory of God, in the power of the Holy Spirit. No longer are we going to be wimpy people. It is not who we are! Don't give into the flesh any longer. It is not who we are. You are powerful! Do not let the enemy define you, let your Bridegroom define you!

WEDDINGS OF ANCIENT ISRAEL
A PICTURE OF MESSIAH
AND HIS BRIDE

1) The Shiddukhin: Arrangements preliminary to betrothal
   Isaiah 62:5, Ephesians 1:3: The Father chooses an acceptable bride for His worthy Son

2) The Ketubah: "The marriage covenant"
   Ephesians 5:22–32: The marriage covenant between the husband and wife reflects the covenant with Christ and His Bride

3) The Mohar: The Bridal Payment
   1 Corinthians 6:19–20, 1 Peter 2:18–19: Jesus gave his life, paying the redemptive price for our sin

4) The Mikveh: Ritual Immersion
   Matthew 3:13–15, Matthew 28:18–20: Jesus was baptized to fulfill all righteousness, believers are baptized in obedience to Christ

5) The Eyrusin: Betrothal
   a) The Covenantal Vows (Matthew 26:26–28), The Last Supper
   b) The Cup seals the Covenant (Matthew 26:29), Jesus shares the cup of wine and promises not to drink this cup again until He is in the Father's kingdom.

c) The Bridegroom goes away to build a home for his bride and promises to return (John 14:1–2).
d) The Bride prepares herself for the bridegroom's return. She does not know the day or the hour of his return. She is consecrated and waits patiently and expectantly for her Bridegroom's return (Matthew 25:12).
e) His return is Imminent (Titus 2:11–13).

6) The Matan: The Bridal Gift
Ephesians 4:7: Jesus purchased spiritual gifts for His bride.

7) The Bridegroom's Return:
a) 1 Thessalonians 4:13–18: The bridegroom snatches the bride away.
b) The bridegroom takes her to his wedding chamber for seven days. Daniel 9:24–27: Daniel's seventieth week with is the time of Jacob's trouble. This week is symbolic of the seven-year tribulation period (Revelation 4:1–4).

8) The Marriage Supper
a) After seven days in the wedding chamber, the Bridegroom introduces his wife to the guests, when they will celebrate the wedding feast (Matthew 19:6–9).
b) The Bridegroom is Jesus: 2 Corinthians 11:2, Ephesians 5:22–32
c) The Bride is the church: 2 Corinthians 11:2; Ephesians 5:22–32 Revelation 21:9–10.
d) The guests are those saved during the tribulation period: Matthew 25:1–10.

9) Co-Reigning
The husband and wife co-reign in the home with the husband as the head of the wife. Revelation 4:1–4, 19:11–16, Jesus

comes to earth with His bride, the armies of heaven and rule and reign with Him during the millennial kingdom.

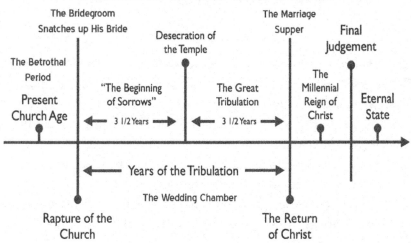

The Wedding Chamber
Christ with His Bride

Seven Days in the Wedding Chamber

Ancient Jewish eschatology taught that a seven-year "time of Jacob's trouble" that would come upon the earth before the coming of the Messiah. During that time of trouble, the righteous would be resurrected and would enter the wedding chamber where they would be protected. Today that seven year period is referred to as the Tribulation. After seven years in Heaven, the Groom, Christ, will bring His wife to Earth and at the time of His Second Coming He will introduce her to the community on Earth.

ABOUT THE AUTHOR

Chris Hussey is the senior pastor of Abundant Life Community Church. He has ministered there for almost twenty-two years. He was born again in August of 1983 at twenty-five years of age. At thirty, he left the sheet metal business to attend Bible College and later went on to receive a master's degree. He has been in the ministry since 1988. However, in 2001, the wind of the Holy Spirit blew in his heart. From that moment on, Chris radically pursued God's presence and power. He has been zealously and intimately been pursuing his Bridegroom, the Lord Jesus. This book flows from the intimacy of that relationship.